TALES OF OLD
SAN FRANCISCO

The rich past of America's most magical city

Graham Earnshaw

"Isn't it nice that people who prefer
Los Angeles to San Francisco
live there?"

Herb Caen

EARNSHAW
BOOKS

Tales of Old San Francisco

By Graham Earnshaw

ISBN-13: 978-988-8273-25-6

This book has been reset in 10pt Book Antiqua. Spellings and punctuations are left as in the original edition.

BISAC HIS036140 / HISTORY / California History

EB071

Published by Earnshaw Books Ltd. (Hong Kong)

The Tales Books

The concept of our Tales series of books is "history with all the juicy bits highlighted and all the boring bits removed," a curated and easily digestible pot pourri of historical oddities, stories and information from a city's past. A pastiche of quotes, extracts and old images, with some explanation along the way. It is a selective choice and somewhat random, certainly not completist. The material is laid out roughly chronologically, but you can open the book anywhere and start reading. Historical cliches are revived and addressed with glee. Virtually nothing strays over two pages. Please enjoy the feast.

The materials in the book come from a myriad sources. If any item is attributed inappropriately, please let us know and we will correct it. We believe all materials are either out of copyright or used within the bounds of fair usage. We are happy to remove any items where this proves not to be the case.

Other Books in the Tales Series

Tales of Old Shanghai
Tales of Old Hong Kong
Tales of Old Peking
Tales of Old Singapore
Tales of Old Batavia
Tales of Old Tokyo
Tales of Old Tianjin
Tales of Old Hainan
Tales of Old Manila

Chronology

3000 BC	First humans move to the Bay area
1769	Portola expedition visits region, the first Westerners to see the Bay (assuming Francis Drake never entered).
1776	Juan Bautiza de Anza marches north from San Diego with a settlement party to establish a Spanish presidio and the Mission San Francisco de Asis
1821	Mexico wins independence from Spain
1835	An American, William Richardson, becomes the first permanent resident of Yerba Buena.
1846, June	"California Republic" is declared
1846, July 9	US Navy captain James B. Montgomery raises the U.S. flag in Yerba Buena's plaza (today's Portsmouth Square), claiming the region for the United States.
1847	Settlement's name is changed from Yerba Buena to San Francisco
1848, January 24	The first gold is discovered at Sutter's Fort in today's Sacramento, 90 miles northeast of San Francisco
1859	Silver boom in Nevada's Comstock Lode results in another boom for San Francisco
1865	*San Francisco Chronicle* is founded
1868	University of California, Berkeley is founded
1906, April 18	Earthquake and subsequent fires destroy much of the city, killing 3,000 people

1933	San Francisco Ballet is founded
1934	West Coast Waterfront strikes
1937	Golden Gate Bridge opens
1942	Japanese residents are interned
1945	San Francisco hosts the conference estabishing the United Nations
1946	The 49ers football team is founded
1951	Jack Kerouac arrives in San Francisco
1958	The Giants baseball team relocates to San Francisco
1965	The Grateful Dead play their first concert
1967	The "Summer of Love," marking the high point of the hippie counterculture
1972	The Transamerica Pyramid tower is completed
1978	Harvey Milk is assassinated
1980	First AIDS case is reported (Ken Horne)
1989	Loma Prieta earthquake rattles northern California

San Francisco in 1851, at the start of the Gold Rush

Introduction

San Francisco's rich and varied past unfolded in such a short period of history that it is nearly impossible to comprehensively digest. The city has played a crucial role in so many moments and movements that it becomes almost impossible to try to sum up all of the elements in a single book. But we will try to at least hit the high points.

The city on the west coast of North America has been an icon, a leader, a cultural catalyst, a beacon of hope, a cauldron of creativity, and a melting pot of diversity. For much of the late 19th century, San Fransisco was a metaphor for the "end of the Earth," like Timbuktu, or the Back of Bourke. Interestingly enough, the Chinese played as much of a role in defining San Francisco's personality as the Anglo-Saxons, and the Irish, Italian fishermen, Spanish priests, Mexican traders, Japanese shop-keepers and South Sea migrants all made a contribution

and left a mark on it.

There is a definite magic about San Francisco that many of the people quoted herein refer to. Its harbor and hills, its fogs and free spirit.

San Francisco was a mecca for adventurers in the mid-19th and again in the mid-20th century. From gold bars to gold records, it has captured the imagination of generations, and continues to cast a shadow far wider than its size and the length of its history should warrant.

The period covered by this book starts in time immemorial and ends in the 1970s. There is no absolute clear line for dividing old San Francisco from modern San Francisco, but we have in mind 1975 as a rough cut-off point.

The area around what is today called San Francisco Bay was for many thousands of years the quiet home for no more than a few thousand Native Americans who lived an idyllic life in an enchanted and isolated land. Then came the Spanish and the Mexicans, who established small settlements and Catholic ministry outposts called missions in many parts of what is today California. In the 1840s, the Americans from the eastern side of the continent finally made their way to the coast of northern Californian, with the US flag being raised at what is today Portsmouth Square in the city of San Francisco in 1847.

The following year, the great California gold rush began. In just a few months, San Francisco was transformed from an anonymous backwater to an international mecca. For the next few decades, the city was the link point between California's vast goldfields and the global market.

The city experienced scandalous and exhilarating booms followed by devestating busts, establishing itself as one of the world's most important transport hubs and cosmopolitan metropolises. San Frasisco rapidly became a cultural melting pot, harboring for a time the largest communities of Chinese, Italian, Mexican, and Japanese immigrants in America.

San Francisco played an extraordinarily important role in terms of World War II and was the point of embarkation for a large proportion of the American troops who fought the Japanese in the Pacific Theatre between 1941 and 1945.

Then came the Beat era, in the 1950s, when a generation of outcasts from elsewhere in the United States gathered to create a cultural revolution based on poetry, music and lifestyle, all alternative, often outrageous and with a lasting impact on both American and global culture.

San Francisco's role in nurturing the Beat Generation was, however, just the beginning of the citie's impact on the global conscience. In the 1960s, the city jumped to the top of the ranks of globally significant cities yet again when it became the launching pad for the hippie generation, with music taking a leading role thanks to rock bands such as the Grateful Dead and Jefferson Airplane.

In the 1970s, San Francisco led the way in yet another revolution. The gay rights movement in America found a certain degree of sanctuary in San Francisco, the city serving as a safe haven for what at the time was a persecuted lifestyle in many parts of America.

Many writers have commented on the unique mixture of cultures existing in San Francisco, and the sharp differences between the city and the general culture of the United States. It has sometimes been referred to in recent decades as the "People's Republic of San Francisco," thanks to the generally liberal views of its inhabitants. For the rest of America, San Fransisco seems to exists not only as a different city, but also as a different universe. Vive La Difference.

Graham Earnshaw
October 2017

San Francisco Chinatown

Pre-History

It is generally believed today that the ancestors of the Native Americans, including the Ohlone people who inhabited the region around San Francisco Bay, traveled from northern Asia across the Bering Strait around 20,000 years ago. The forebears of the people that Europeans first met in the area appear to have moved in around 6,000 years ago. The Spanish, who set up small settlements in the 17th century, called these people Costanoans, but the term Ohlone has been generally preferred since the 1970s. It was estimated that there were between 10,000 and 20,000 residents of the region divided into 50 tribes or groups, each with varying languages and customs. They hunted and fished in the area until the 1770s, but with the Spanish came disaster. Franciscan missions were established to "civilize" the native peoples and convert them to Christianity. The local people were generally required to move to the Missions to live and work, and their numbers declined sharply largely due to epidemics. In 1794 and 1795, "a total of 81,000 Indians were baptized and 60,000 deaths were recorded." Today, the Muwekma Ohlone Tribe has as its members descendants of the Ohlones from the region.

A postcard issued for the 1939-1940 Golden Gate International Exposition

Drake and the Spaniards

The English seafarer Sir Francis Drake, the second captain ever to circumnavigate the globe, sighted northern California in 1579, but it appears he never sailed through the Golden Gates into San Francisco Bay. He named the region New Albion, claiming it in the name of Queen Elizabeth. The exact place he landed was a closely guarded secret, for fear of the Spanish finding out, but it is believed to be Drake's Bay, about 30 miles northwest of the Golden Gate passage. In the late 19th century, the area was the home to a fishing fleet run by immigrants from Naples.

It was nearly 200 years before another European made it to this part of the world. That was the Spanish explorer Gaspar de Portolà on November 4, 1769, who sighted the bay from a mountain top while looking for Monterey. And then another six years passed before the first European ship entered San Francisco Bay. Spaniard Juan de Ayala sailed through the Golden Gate on August 5, 1775 in his ship the San Carlos. They docked at what is now Ayala Cove, and gave names to several locations, including Alcatraz Island. In 1846, the United States went to war with Mexico and used the opportunity to seize California, which formally became part of the United States with the signing of the Treaty of Guadalupe Hidalgo in February 1848. California became the 31st state of the Union on September 9, 1850.

A camp in San Francisco in the early days of the Gold Rush

The USS San Francisco, a cruiser launched in 1889, and sold for scrap in 1939. The ship served in the Spanish-American war, and was involved in mine-laying in the North Sea during World War I to stop German submarines

A late 19th century bird's eye view

The Mission

The Mission San Francisco de Asís is the oldest surviving structure in the city of San Francisco. The Mission was established in June, 1776 by Lieutenant José Joaquin Moraga and Father Francisco Palóu, members of the de Anza Expedition which opened up Alta California to Spanish settlers while also working to convert the local Native American residents to Christianity.

> Leaving San Francisco is like saying goodbye to an old sweetheart.
> You want to linger as long as possible.
> *Walter Cronkite*

The Presidio

The Presidio is a former military based on the northern tip of the San Francisco peninsula. It was set up by the Spanish in 1776 to cement their control of the entire region, and they called it El Presidio Real de San Francisco or The Royal Fortress of Saint Francis. When Mexico gained its independence, it passed into Mexican hands, and was seized by United States forces only in 1846.

The Presidio was involved in most of America's military activities in the Pacific and further west. It was the assembly point for the US Army forces that invaded the Philippines in the Spanish-American War of 1898, and the headquarters for defense of the Western United States during World War II. The order to intern Japanese-Americans during World War II was signed at the Presidio. On its closure in 1995, the Presidio was the longest continuously operated military base in the country.

The Morning Salute at the Presidio of San Francisco

Salt and Taxes

A excerpt from Mark Kurlansky's history of the substance salt, entitled Salt, *and published in 2002.*

The southern end of San Francisco Bay is an insalubrious marshland with ideal conditions for salt making. Not only does it have more sun and less rainfall than San Francisco and the north bay, but it has wind to help with evaporation. The intensely hot air from central California comes over the mountains, and the temperature difference sucks in the cool sea breeze. This is why centuries and perhaps millennia before the California and Nevada silver strikes, a people called the Ohlone made annual pilgrimages to this area for salt making. At the water's edge, the brine slowly evaporated in the sun and wind and left a thick layer of salt crystals. They had only to scrape it. The first European to notice the local salt making was a Spanish priest, Jose Danti, who explored the eastern side of the bay in 1795. In the southern end of the east bay, he found marshes with thick layers of salt, and "the natives," he reported, told him that it provided salt for much of the area. The Spanish were content to let the Ohlone produce salt. They only wanted a share-a very large one-of the profits.

A real estate map of San Francisco in 1890

Naming San Francisco

An announcement from Washington Bartlett, the Chief Magistrate of the town, issued on January 30, 1847 formalizing the city's name.

AN ORDINANCE WHEREAS, the local name of Yerba Buena, as applied to the settlement or town of San Francisco, is unknown beyond the district; and has been applied from the local name of the cove, on which the town is built: Therefore, to prevent confusion and mistakes in public documents, and that the town may have the advantage of the name given on the public map;

IT IS HEREBY ORDAINED, that the name of SAN FRANCISCO shall hereafter be used in all official communications and public documents, or records appertaining to the town.

What's In A Name?

No one today knows what the native American residents of the San Francisco area called it. Maybe just home. The whole region was named Alta California (upper California) by the Spanish when they claimed it all in the 18th century, and the first European settlement in the area was called Yerba Buena, at least that was the name of the Mission established by the Spanish and the Franciscan monks who trailed after them. The name was changed to San Francisco after the whole region was seized by the United States as part of its war with Mexico. And so it has remained.

The Chinese residents of San Francisco have been an important part of the cultural landscape of the city right from the beginning of the Gold Rush in 1848-49. They called it GauGamSaan - "old gold mountain" in Cantonese - the Cantonese dominated the Chinese community for more than a century. Hong Kong Chinese changed their name for the city to SaamFaanSee - a transliteration of the first two syllables of the English name, plus "see" meaning "city". But for mainland China-origin residents, it remains today as Old Gold Mountain.

The city's name in English is sometimes abbreviated to Frisco, sometimes with a preceding apostrophe, and sometimes not. The San Francisco Chronicle columnist Herb Caen, who finally hung up his typewriter ribbon in 1997, considered this term to be demeaning and railed vigorously against its use. He even wrote a book in 1953 entitled *Don't Call It Frisco*. In his honor, we won't.

A name for San Francisco in Chinese - Old Gold Mountain

Another name for the city in Chinese - Three (San) Fan City

17

The Forty-Niners

One of the best accounts of the fever that overtook the United States in 1849 on the news of gold discoveries in the mountains around San Francisco is that of Daniel Knower, whose memoir entitled The Adventures of a Forty-Niner *was published in 1894. He sailed on a ship from New York with a quantity of lumber to take advantage of what he understood to be desperate shortage of house-building materials in San Francisco. Here is an extract about a deal gone wrong:*

At the time of my arrival, on August 18, 1849, there were several hundreds of ships anchored in the bay deserted by their crews, who had gone to the mines. They could make more in one day there than their wages would amount to in a month on the vessel.

In the city a large portion of its population were living in tents. There were not buildings enough. Vessels were constantly arriving loaded with people from all parts of the world. As my health permitted I investigated matters there. I took a walk out. I met what looked like a laboring man. I asked him how long he had been there? He said two months. I said to him: "And not gone up to the mines yet?" He said to me he was in no particular hurry. He said he had a row-boat and made $20 a day rowing passengers to and from the vessels (there was then no dock). He had his boy with him, who gathered mussels and sold them. Between the two they averaged $30 per day, which explained why he was in no hurry to go to the gold diggings.

Lumber was bringing fabulous prices. It looked very favorable for my house ventures. Mr. G., the Englishman, had been very anxious to buy them. He had seen the specifications of the carpenter on the steamer coming up. On Saturday P.M. I called at his office. He asked me if I had made up my mind to sell him the houses. I said to him: "If I should put a price on them you would not take me up." He said "try me." I named a price. He said he would take them and go to my lawyer to draw up the contract. I said I would just as soon go to his (which was a fatal mistake). I knew his was a State senator from Florida, and had come up on the steamer with us. We found the lawyer in his office, and he commenced drawing up the contract. I made my statement that I sold the houses from my carpenter's specifications (not from any representations I made myself), and from the bills of lading and from my insurance policy, which ranked the ship Prince de Joinville, formerly a Havre packet, classed A, No. 1. He was to deposit bills of lading of the ship St. George from Liverpool, consigned to him, in value to the amount of $50,000, with a third party, as collateral security, that on the arrival of the Prince de Joinville, and the delivery of the houses, he was to pay me the sum agreed upon.

The lawyer, after writing a little, complained of a headache, and asked if it made any difference if he put it off until Monday morning. I said, Mr. G. had been very anxious to buy the houses, and I had not cared about selling them to arrive, preferring to take my chances when the vessel got here, but since I had consented to sell them, I preferred to have it on the solid. I said, I supposed the transaction was not of great importance to Mr. G., but I had all that I was worth in the world at stake on the venture, and would prefer to have it closed now. He commenced writing, and again complained of the headache. I then consented to put it off until Monday morning at 10 o'clock. We both pledged our honor to meet there at that time and consummate it. I was there on Monday morning at the time designated. Mr. G. came in at 11 o'clock and said he had changed his mind and would not take the houses. I said all right, but his word of pledge of honor would have no value with me hereafter.

A Spark In the Fog

A wonderful description by writer Bayard Taylor of San Francisco just as it exploded into a city in 1849. From his book Eldorado, *or* Adventures in the Path of Empire, *published in 1850.*

The appearance of San Francisco at night, from the water, is unlike anything I ever beheld. The houses are mostly of canvas, which is made transparent by the lamps within. and transforms them, in the darkness, to dwellings of solid light. Seated on the slopes of its three hills, the tents pitched among the chaparral to the very summits, it gleams like an amphitheatre of fire. Here and there shine out brilliant points, from the decoy-lamps of the gaming-houses; and through the indistinct murmur of the streets comes by fits the sound of music from their hot and crowded precincts. The picture has in it something unreal and fantastic; it impresses one like the cities of the magic lantern, which a moving of the hand can build or annihilate.

When I had climbed the last sand-hill, riding in towards San Francisco, and the town and harbour and crowded shipping again opened to the view, I could scarcely realize the change that had taken place during my absence of three weeks. The town had not only greatly extended its limits, but seemed actually to have doubled its number of dwellings since I left. High

Cable car turntable on Powell Street

up on the hills, where I had seen only sand and chaparral, stood clusters of houses; streets which had been merely laid out, were hemmed in with buildings and thronged with people; new warehouses had sprung up on the water side, and new piers were creeping out toward the shipping; the forest of masts had greatly thickened; and the noise, motion, and bustle of business and labour on all sides were incessant. Verily, the place was in itself a marvel. To say that it was daily enlarged by from twenty to thirty houses may not sound very remarkable after all the stories that have been told; yet this, for a country which imported both lumber and houses, and where labor was then $10 a day, is an extraordinary growth. The rapidity with which a ready-made house is put up and inhabited, strikes the stranger in San Francisco as little short of magic. He walks over an open-lot in his before-breakfast stroll - the next morning, a house complete, with a family inside, blocks up his way. He goes down to the bay and looks out on the shipping - two or three days afterward a row of storehouses, staring him in the face, intercepts the view.

I went on deck, in the misty daybreak, to take a parting look at the town and its amphitheatric hills. As I turned my face shorewards, a little spark appeared through the fog. Suddenly it shot up into a spiry flame, and at the same instant I heard the sound of gongs, bells and trumpets, and the shouting of human voices. The calamity, predicted and dreaded so long in advance, that men ceased to think of it, had come at last - San Francisco was on fire! The blaze increased with fearful rapidity. In fifteen minutes, it had risen into a broad, flickering column, making all the shore, the misty air and the water ruddy as with another sunrise. The sides of new frame houses, scattered through the town, tents high up on the hills, and the hulls and listless sails of vessels in the bay, gleamed and sparkled in the thick atmosphere. Meanwhile the roar and tumult swelled, and above the clang of gongs and the cries of the populace, I could hear the crackling of blazing timbers, and the smothered sound of falling roofs. I climbed into the rigging and watched the progress of the conflagra-tion. As the flames leaped upon a new dwelling, there was a sudden whirl of their waving volumes an embracing of the frail walls in their relentless clasp - and, a second afterwards, from roof and rafter and foundation beam shot upwards a jet of fire, steady and intense at first, but surging off into spiral folds and streamers, as the timbers were parted and fell.

When you get tired of walking around San Francisco, you can always lean against it.
Transworld Getaway Guide, *San Francisco*, 1975-6

A painting by George Henry Burgess of San Francisco in 1849, at the beginning of the Gold Rush

Piers 29 and 31

His Majesty, the Emperor of the United States

Joshua Abraham Norton, born in England in 1817 or the following year, landed in San Francsco in 1849 and ten years later proclaimed himself to be "Norton I, Emperor of the United States" and also subsequently "Protector of Mexico." He of course had no political power and was a typical eccentric, but he was widely treated with respect in San Francisco. He issued various orders during his reign, including one calling for the dissolution of the US Congress. He collapsed and died on the street in January 1880 and more than 30,000 people attended his funeral.

We're crazy about this city. First time we came here, we walked the streets all day, all over town and nobody hassled us. People smiled, friendly-like, and we knew we could live here. We'd like to keep our place in Greenwich Village and have an apartment here, God and the Immigration Service willing.
John Lennon

Unknown And Watery Graves

Ulysses S. Grant, the 18th president of the United States from 1869 to 1877 and the general commanding the Union forces in the Civil War that ended in 1865, wrote his Personal Memoirs just before his death in 1885. He described San Francisco in both 1852 and 1853, a period of breakneck speed development for the city. Here is his description of San Francisco in 1852:

San Francisco at that day was a lively place. Gold, or placer digging as it was called, was at its height. Steamers plied daily between San Francisco and both Stockton and Sacramento. Passengers and gold from the southern mines came by the Stockton boat; from the northern mines by Sacramento. In the evening when these boats arrived, Long Wharf--there was but one wharf in San Francisco in 1852--was alive with people crowding to meet the miners as they came down to sell their "dust" and to "have a time." Of these some were runners for hotels, boarding houses or restaurants; others belonged to a class of impecunious adventurers, of good manners and good presence, who were ever on the alert to make the acquaintance of people with some ready means, in the hope of being asked to take a meal at a restaurant. Many were young men of good family, good education and gentlemanly instincts. Their parents had been able to support them during their minority, and to give them good educations, but not to maintain them afterwards. From 1849 to 1853 there was a rush of people to the Pacific coast, of the class described. All thought that fortunes were to be picked up, without effort, in the gold fields on the Pacific. Some realized more than their most sanguine expectations; but for one such there were hundreds disappointed, many of whom now fill unknown graves; others died wrecks of their former selves, and many, without a vicious instinct, became criminals and outcasts. Many of the real scenes in early California life exceed in strangeness and interest any of the mere products of the brain of the novelist.

And in 1853...

... I was obliged to remain in San Francisco for several days before I found a vessel. This gave me a good opportunity of comparing the San Francisco of 1852 with that of 1853. As before stated, there had been but one wharf in front of the city in 1852 — Long Wharf. In 1853 the town had grown out into the bay beyond what was the end of this wharf when I first saw it. Streets and houses had been built out on piles where the year before the largest vessels visiting the port lay at anchor or tied to the wharf. There was no filling under the streets or houses. San Francisco presented the same general appearance as the year before; that is, eating, drinking and gambling houses were conspicuous for their number and publicity. They were on the first floor, with doors wide open.

At all hours of the day and night in walking the streets, the eye was regaled, on every block near the water front, by the sight of players at faro. Often broken places were found in the street, large enough to let a man down into the water below. I have but little doubt that many of the people who went to the Pacific coast in the early days of the gold excitement, and have never been heard from since, or who were heard from for a time and then ceased to write, found watery graves beneath the houses or streets built over San Francisco Bay.

Besides the gambling in cards there was gambling on a larger scale in city lots. These were sold "On Change," much as stocks are now sold on Wall Street. Cash, at time of purchase, was always paid by the broker; but the purchaser had only to put up his margin. He was charged at the rate of two or three per cent. a month on the difference, besides commissions. The sand hills, some of them almost inaccessible to foot-passengers, were surveyed off and mapped into fifty vara lots--a vara being a Spanish yard. These were sold at first at very low prices, but were sold and resold for higher prices until they went up to many thousands of dollars. The brokers did a fine business, and so did many such purchasers as were sharp enough to quit purchasing before the final crash came. As the city grew, the sand hills back of the town furnished material for filling up the bay under the houses and streets, and still further out. The temporary houses, first built over the water in the harbor, soon gave way to more solid structures. The main business part of the city now is on solid ground, made where vessels of the largest class lay at anchor in the early days. I was in San Francisco again in 1854. Gambling houses had disappeared from public view. The city had become staid and orderly.

Grant photographed working on his memoirs a month before he died in April, 1885

25

> You can take the girl out of Chinatown but you can't take
> Chinatown out of the girl.
> *Anon.*

Mint Condition

The mountains of gold mined in the Gold Rush starting in 1848-49 had to be absorbed into the financial system somehow, and so in 1850, President Millard Fillmore approved the construction of a mint in San Francisco. It started producing gold coins in 1854, and the classical Grecian style building was opened in 1874. It occupies an entire city block bounded by Fifth Street to the east, Mission Street to the south, Jessie Street to the north, and Mint Street to the west. It survived the 1906 earthquake pretty much unscathed, and still stands today, although it is no longer used to produce currency.

1046   U. S. Mint, Cor. Fifth and Mission Streets, San Francisco, California.

The US Mint on Mission Street

Central San Francisco in the aftermath of the 1906 earthquake and fires

Crucibles Cracked

An excerpt from English writer Frank Marryat's 1855 travel book, California Mountains and Molehills *describing arrival in San Francisco in 1850 just after a fire had ripped through the shanty town.*

We have arrived at the moment of the great June Fire of 1850, and San Francisco is again in ashes--although four hundred houses have been destroyed, they were but of wood or thin sheet iron, and the `devouring element' has made a clean sweep of everything, except a few brick chimneys and iron pots.

Everybody seems to be in good humour--so soon as the embers cool, the work of rebuilding will commence. I found it amusing the next day to walk over the ground and observe the effects of the intense heat on the articles which were strewed around. Gun-barrels were twisted and knotted like snakes; there were tons of nails welded together by the heat, standing in the shape of the kegs which had contained them; small lakes of molten glass of all the colours of the rainbow; tools of all descriptions from which the wood-work had disappeared, and pitch-pots filled with melted lead and glass. Here was an iron house that had collapsed with the heat, and even an iron fire-proof safe that had burst under the same influence; spoons, knives, forks and crockery were melted up together in heaps; crucibles even had cracked; preserved meats had been unable to stand this second cooking, and had exploded in every direction. The loss was very great by this fire, as the houses destroyed had been for the most part filled with merchandise; but there was little time wasted in lamentation, the energy of the people showed itself at once in action, and in forty-eight hours after the fire the whole district resounded to the din of busy workmen.

A street scene in 1850s San Francisco

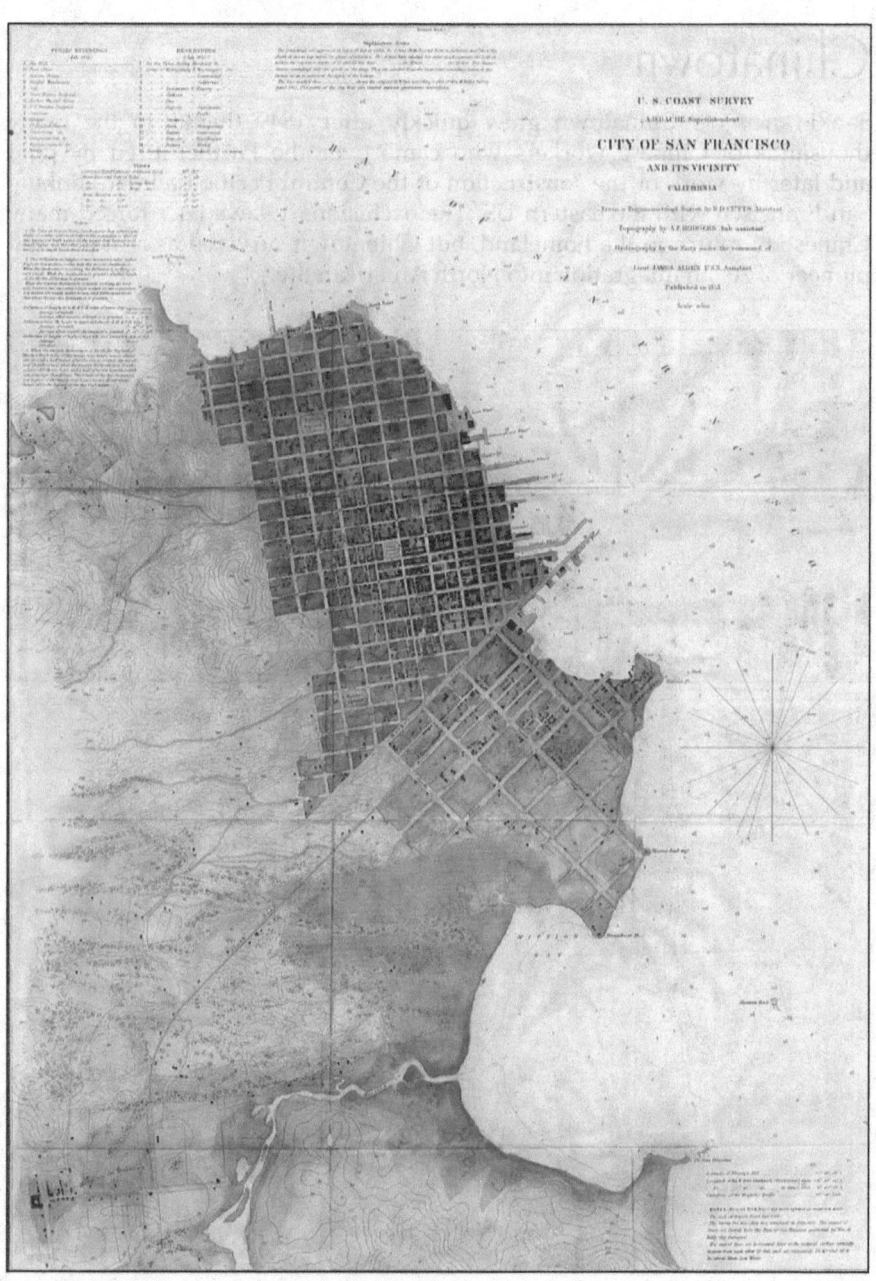

Chinatown

San Francisco's Chinatown grew quickly after 1849 thanks to the many thousands of Chinese workers who came over the Pacific, lured by gold and later by work or the construction of the Central Pacific Railroad, linking San Francisco with the eastern US. The exclusionary laws later forced many Chinese to return to the homeland, but Chinatown survived as a model and pioneer of Asian integration into North American life.

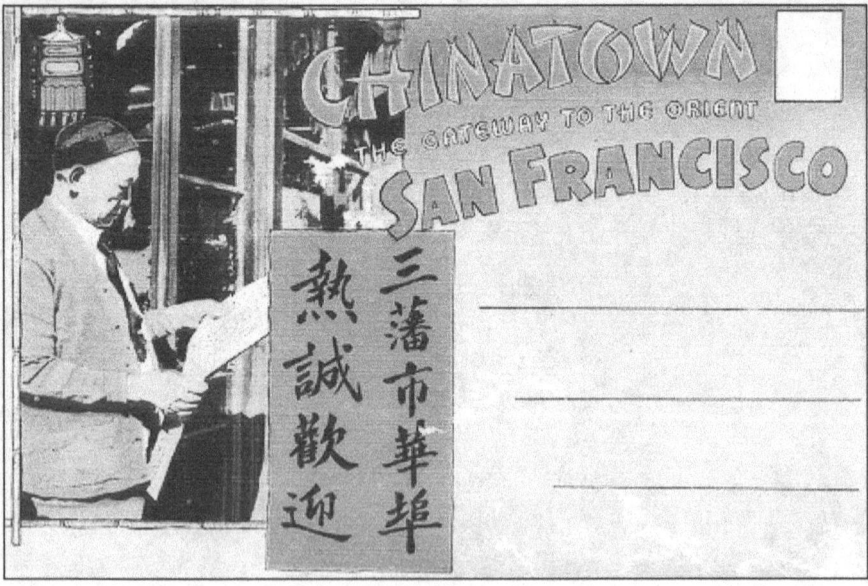

Shanghai-ed in San Francisco

San Francisco was a difficult port for ship captains and owners, particularly in the 1850s and 1860s. Crew members would often just disappear once the ship docked and go to seek their fortunes in the gold fields, leaving the ships with insufficient crew members to set sail again. They often resolved the problem by kidnapping sailors while they were drinking in the bars of the Barbary Coast, a tenderloin district of San Francisco named after a particularly lawless region in North Africa. Some of the drinking establishments in San Francisco's Barbary Coast were actually built on stilts over the waters of the Bay, and according to legend, the sailors would be given spiked drinks, and then be tipped unconscious into boats waiting down below. When they awoke, they found themselves on a whaler heading out to sea, probably for months in the waters of Alaska or the South Pacific.

"Do You Feel Lucky ... Punk?"

San Francisco has starred in many movies, but none of them so memorable as the Dirty Harry series starring Clint Eastwood as a detective trying to clean up the city by scaring the criminals to death. The first film features a whole list of classic San Francisco locations including City Hall, the Golden Gate Park and the iconic Bank of America Building.

Detective Harry Callahan.

You don't assign him to murder cases.

You just turn him loose.

**Clint Eastwood
Dirty Harry**

Interesting Specimens

Charles A. Murdock first visited San Francisco in 1855, moving there to live in 1864 and building a highly respected printing business. His memoir, A Backward Glance at Eighty, *was published in 1921.*

Let the diary tell the tale of the beginning of life in California: "I arose about 4-1/2 this morning and went on deck. We were then in the Golden Gate, which is the entrance into San Francisco Bay. On each side of us was high land. On the left-hand side was a lighthouse, and the light was still burning. On my right hand was the outer telegraph building. When they see us they telegraph to another place, from which they telegraph all over San Francisco. When we were going in there was a strong ebb tide. We arrived at the wharf a little after five o'clock. The first thing which I did was to look for my father. Him I did not see."

Father had been detained in Humboldt by the burning of the connecting steamer, so we went to Wilson's Exchange in Sansome near Sacramento Street, and in the afternoon took the "Senator" for Sacramento, where my uncle and aunt lived.

The part of a day in San Francisco was used to the full in prospecting the strange city. We walked its streets and climbed its hills, much interested in all we saw. The line of people waiting for their mail up at Portsmouth Square was perhaps the most novel sight. A race up the bay, waiting for the tide at Benicia,

117-LOMBARD STREET, CROOKEDEST STREET IN THE WORLD
SAN FRANCISCO, CALIFORNIA

sticking on the "Hog's Back" in the night, and the surprise of a flat, checkerboard city were the most impressive experiences of the trip to Sacramento.

A month or so on this compulsory visit passed very pleasantly. We found fresh delight in watching the Chinese and their habits. We had never seen a specimen before. A very pleasant picnic and celebration on the Fourth of July was another attractive novelty. Cheap John auctions and frequent fires afforded amusement and excitement, and we learned to drink muddy water without protest.

> "To a traveler paying his first visit, it has the interest of a new planet. It ignores the meteorological laws which govern the rest of the world."
> *Fitz Hugh Ludlow, best known for his autobiographical book* The Hasheesh Eater, *published in 1857 when he was 21 years old.*

A Boeing 314 Clipper flying over San Francisco, 1940

> My San Francisco on her seven hills is smiling, beside an opalescent sunset sea.
> *George Caldwell*

The Glimmer of White Tent Tops

This is the beginning of a romantic mystery novel published in 1909 called The Other Side of the Door *written by Lucia Chamberlain. It was set in the year 1865. Here is how she describes San Francisco at that time:*

The city is always gray. Even in March, the greenest month of all, when the Presidio, and the Mission Hills, and the islands in the bay are beautiful with spring, there's only such a little bit of green gets into the city! It lies in the lap of five hills, climbing upward toward their crests where the trees are all doubled and bent by the trade-wind. It seems to give its own color to the growing things in it. The cypress hedges are dusty black; the eucalyptus trees are gray as the house fronts they knock against, and even the plaza grass looks dark and old, as if it had been the same grass always, and never came up new in the spring.

But for the most part there are no trees, and only the finest places have gardens. There are only rows and rows of houses painted gray, with here and there a white one, or a glass conservatory front. But the fog and dust all summer gray these, too, and when the trade-winds blow hard it takes the smoke out over the east bay, and makes that as gray as the city.

And yet the city doesn't look sad. The sky is too blue, and the bay is too blue around it; and the flying fog, and the wind, and the strong tide flowing in and out of the bay are like restless, eager creatures that never sleep or grow tired. When I was a very little child the fierceness of it frightened me. All the noises of the city made one harsh, threatening voice to my ears; and the perilous water encompassing far as eye could reach; and the high hills running up into the sky now blinded by dust, now buried in fog, now drenched in rain, were overpowering and terrifying to me. Beyond that general seeming of terror there is little I remember of the early city, except the glimmer of white tent tops against gray fog or blue water, the loud voices in the streets, and a vague, general impression of rapid and violent changes of place and circumstance.

A poem by Bret Harte, San Francisco from the Sea, *dating from around 1860*

Serene, indifferent of Fate
Thou sittest at the Western Gate

Upon thy heights so lately won
Still slant the banners of the sun;

Thou seest the white seas strike their tents
O Warder of two Continents! ...

Thou drawest all things, small or great
To thee beside the Western gate.

O Lion's whelp, that hidest fast
In jungle growth of spire and mast

I know thy cunning and thy greed
Thy hard high lust and wilful deed,

And all thy glory loves to tell
Of specious gifts material

Drop down, O fleecy Fog and hide
Her sceptic sneer, and all her pride!

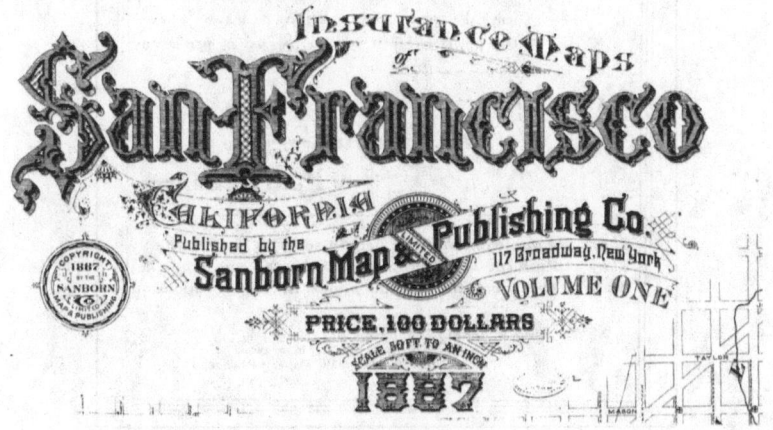

Keeper of the Doors

The Call was a newspaper serving San Francisco that may hold a record for the number of changes in name during its life, largely due to mergers. It was called *The Morning Call* from its establishment in 1856 until 1895. Mark Twain worked on the paper for a time in the 1860s. It was later called *The Call*, the *San Francisco Call*, *The San Francisco Call & Post*, the *San Francisco Call-Bulletin* (1929), the *San Francisco News-Call Bulletin* and the *News-Call Bulletin* (1959) before finally merging with the *San Francisco Examiner* in 1965 and disappearing as a name altogether, though no doubt living on in spirit.

THE BANK OF CALIFORNIA.

SAN FRANCISCO.

CAPITAL   ·   · $5,000,000

D. O. MILLS   ·   ·   PRESIDENT
W. O. RALSTON   -   ·   CASHIER

AGENTS:

New York - MESSRS. LEES & WALLER
Boston - TREMONT NATIONAL BANK
London ORIENTAL BANK CORPORATION

LETTERS OF CREDIT ISSUED, AVAILable for the purchase of Merchandise
throughout the United States, Europe, India,
China, Japan and Australia.

A newspaper advertisement published in 1869 for the Bank of California's San Francisco branch

Get Off My Foot

Charles Earl Bowles, known as Black Bart, was an outlaw born in England who became one of the most famous robbers in California in the 1870s and 1880s. But he was considered a gentleman was noted for leaving poetic messages behind at the scene of some of his robberies. Here is a poem he left in strongbox he robbed in San Francisco:

> "I've labored long and hard for bread,
> For honor and for riches,
> But on my corns too long you've tread,
> You fair-haired sons of bitches."

San Francisco! Is there a land where the magic of that name has not been felt?
Clarence E. Edwords, author of the book. A Bohemian Guide to San Francisco Restaurants, *published in 1914.*

> Few cities create such a wake of expectation as San Francisco. You get the impression that if the place were chosen as the setting for the Second Coming the citizens would be pleased but not surprised.
>
> *Edward Mace, travel editor for the* Observer *newspaper, writing in 1978*

Fog vs. Smoke

Andrew Carnegie, steel magnate from Pittsburgh and one of the world's richest men, traveled round the world in 1878 and 1879, and published a book about his experiences, Around the World, in 1880. Here is his description of San Francisco, with a wise comment on the air quality.

We reached Oakland, the Jersey City of San Francisco, on time to the minute; the ferry-boat starts, and there lies before us the New York of the Pacific: but instead of the bright sparkling city we had pictured, sinking to rest with its tall spires suffused by the glories of the setting sun, imagine our surprise when not even our own smoky Pittsburgh could boast a denser canopy of smoke. A friend who had kindly met us upon arrival at Oakland tried to explain that this was not all smoke; it was mostly fog, and a peculiar wind which sometimes had this effect; but we could scarcely be mistaken upon that point. No, no, Mr. O'B., you may know all about "Frisco," the Chinese, the mines, and the Yosemite, but do allow me to know something about smoke. We reached our hotel, from the seven days' trip, and, after a bath and a good dinner with agreeable company, were shown as much of the city as it was possible to see before the "wee short hour ayont the twal'."

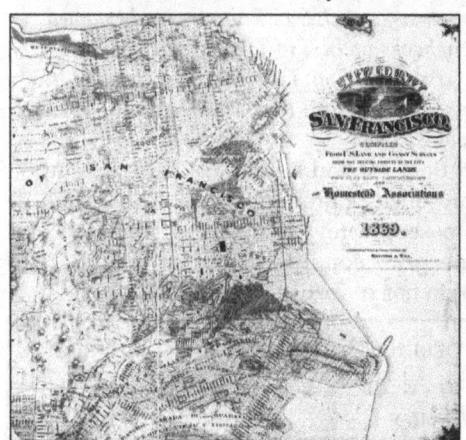

Banking of California Building, opened in 1908

She is not only the most interesting city in the Union, and the hugest smelting-pot of the races and the precious metals. She keeps, besides, the doors of the Pacific, and is port of entry to another world and another epoch in man's history. *From Robert Louis Stevenson's novel*, The Wrecker, *published in 1892.*

The Robert Louis Stevenson memorial in San Francisco's Portsmouth Square commemorates his stay in the city for four months from December 1879, a visit he made to secure the love of a married, though separated, San Francisco lady named Fanny Sitwell. Stevenson, author of many books including Treasure Island, met Fanny in France in 1876. She agreed to go with him, and they married in 1880 in England. Stevenson died in 1894 in Samoa in the South Pacific at the age of 44. The inscription, an excerpt from one of his books, reads:

To be honest, to be kind - to earn a little, to spend a little less - to make upon the whole a family happier for his presence - to renounce when that shall be necessary, and not be embittered - to keep a few friends but these without capitulation - above all on the same grim condition to keep friends with himself - here is a task for all that a man has of fortitude and delicacy.

Break the rules and you go to prison. Break the prison rules and you go to Alcatraz.
Anon.

San Francisco is perhaps the most European of all American cities.
Cecil Beaton, It Gives Me Great Pleasure, 1955.

41

A Great Commercial Emporium

Jules Verne, the French novelist and father of science fiction, published his novel
Around The World in 80 Days in 1873. It featured our British hero, Phileas Fogg
and his French valet Passepartout attempting to circumnavigate the world in 80
days on a £20,000 bet. They naturally passed through San Francisco, and the follow-
ing passage starts as the adventurers disembark from the ship that had carried them
from Yokohama.

It was seven in the morning when Mr. Fogg, Aouda, and Passepartout set foot
upon the American continent, if this name can be given to the floating quay
upon which they disembarked. These quays, rising and falling with the tide,
thus facilitate the loading and unloading of vessels. Alongside them were
clippers of all sizes, steamers of all nationalities, and the steamboats, with
several decks rising one above the other, which ply on the Sacramento and
its tributaries. There were also heaped up the products of a commerce which
extends to Mexico, Chili, Peru, Brazil, Europe, Asia, and all the Pacific islands.

Passepartout, in his joy on reaching at last the American continent, thought
he would manifest it by executing a perilous vault in fine style; but, tumbling
upon some worm-eaten planks, he fell through them.vPut out of countenance
by the manner in which he thus "set foot" upon the New World, he uttered a
loud cry, which so frightened the innumerable cormorants and pelicans that are
always perched upon these movable quays, that they flew noisily away.

Mr. Fogg, on reaching shore, proceeded to find out at what hour the first
train left for New York, and learned that this was at six o'clock p.m.; he had,
therefore, an entire day to spend in the Californian capital. Taking a carriage at
a charge of three dollars, he and Aouda entered it, while Passepartout mounted
the box beside the driver, and they set out for the International Hotel.

From his exalted position Passepartout observed with much curiosity
the wide streets, the low, evenly ranged houses, the Anglo-Saxon Gothic
churches, the great docks, the palatial wooden and brick warehouses, the
numerous conveyances, omnibuses, horse-cars, and upon the side-walks, not
only Americans and Europeans, but Chinese and Indians. Passepartout was
surprised at all he saw. San Francisco was no longer the legendary city of 1849--
a city of banditti, assassins, and incendiaries, who had flocked hither in crowds
in pursuit of plunder; a paradise of outlaws, where they gambled with gold-
dust, a revolver in one hand and a bowie-knife in the other: it was now a great
commercial emporium.

The lofty tower of its City Hall overlooked the whole panorama of the
streets and avenues, which cut each other at right-angles, and in the midst of

which appeared pleasant, verdant squares, while beyond appeared the Chinese quarter, seemingly imported from the Celestial Empire in a toy-box. Sombreros and red shirts and plumed Indians were rarely to be seen; but there were silk hats and black coats everywhere worn by a multitude of nervously active, gentlemanly-looking men. Some of the streets-- especially Montgomery Street, which is to San Francisco what Regent Street is to London, the Boulevard des Italiens to Paris, and Broadway to New York— were lined with splendid and spacious stores, which exposed in their windows the products of the entire world.

When Passepartout reached the International Hotel, it did not seem to him as if he had left England at all. The ground floor of the hotel was occupied by a large bar, a sort of restaurant freely open to all passers-by, who might partake of dried beef, oyster soup, biscuits, and cheese, without taking out their purses. Payment was made only for the ale, porter, or sherry which was drunk. This seemed "very American" to Passepartout. The hotel refreshment-rooms were comfortable, and Mr. Fogg and Aouda, installing themselves at a table, were abundantly served on diminutive plates by negroes of darkest hue.

After breakfast, Mr. Fogg, accompanied by Aouda, started for the English consulate to have his passport visaed. As he was going out, he met Passepartout, who asked him if it would not be well, vbefore taking the train, to purchase some dozens of Enfield rifles and Colt's revolvers. He had been listening to stories of attacks upon the trains by the Sioux and Pawnees. Mr. Fogg thought itva useless precaution, but told him to do as he thought best, and went on to the consulate.

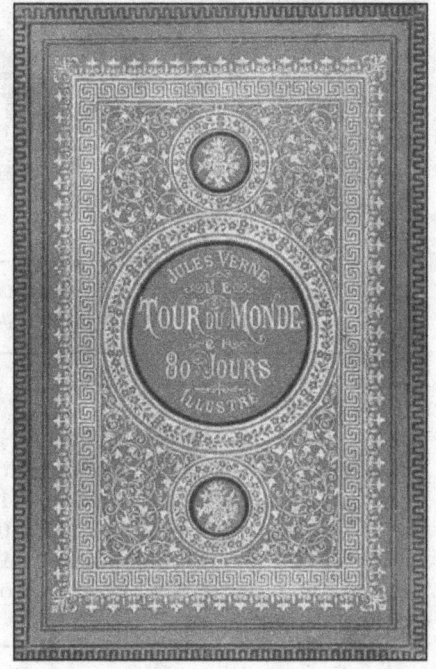

He had not proceeded two hundred steps, however, when, "by the greatest chance in the world," he met Fix. The detective seemed wholly taken by surprise. What! Had Mr. Fogg and himself crossed the Pacific together, and not met on the steamer! At least Fix felt honoured to behold once more the gentleman to whom he owed so much, and, as his business recalled him to Europe, he should be delighted to continue the journey in such pleasant company.

A detail from a postcard dating from around 1900 of the pre-earthquake City Hall, destroyed by fire one day after the earthquake hit on April 18, 1906

Tadich Grill

This is the oldest restaurant in San Francisco, indeed in California. The original establishment opened in 1849 as a coffee stand on Clay Street, and in 1887 John Tadich, a native of Croatia, bought and renamed the restaurant after himself. In 1928, the Buich family bought the restaurant and continue to run it today in a location on California Street that in design terms is true to its predecessor on Clay Street.

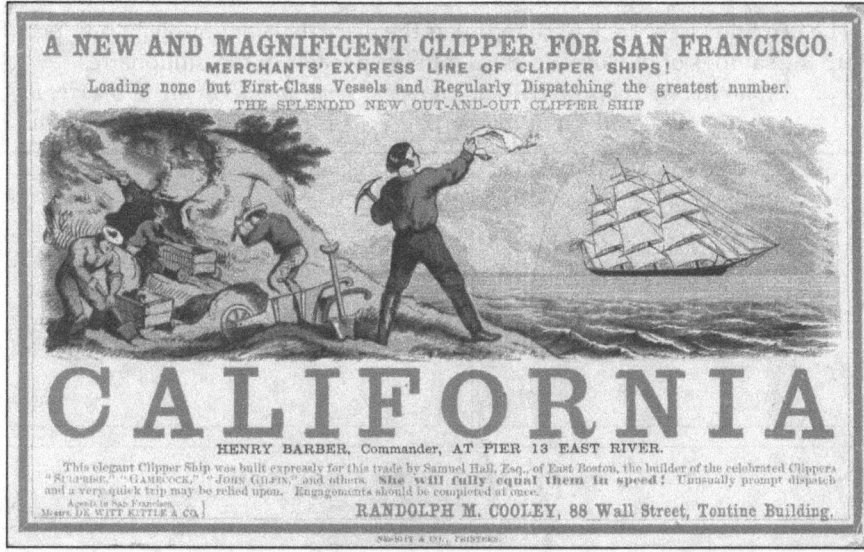

"Perpetual spring, the flare of adventure in the blood, the impulse of men who packed Virgil with their bean-bags on the overland journey, conspired to make San Francisco a city of artists."

William Henry Irwin, American journalist who died in 1948.

Advert from the San Francisco newspaper The Morning Call, *April 1, 1890*

> The San Francisco Stock Exchange was the place that continuously pumped up the savings of the lower classes into the pockets of the millionaires.
>
> *Author Robert Louis Stevenson, who spent some months living in the city in 1880. His comment is, of course, true of every stock exchange.*

The Mingling of the Races

Author Robert Louis Stevenson describing San Francisco in 1883.

Choose a place on one of the huge throbbing ferry-boats, and when you are midway between the city and the suburb, look around. The air is fresh and salt, as if you were at sea. On the one hand is Oakland, gleaming white among its gardens. On the other, to seaward, hill after hill is crowded and crowned with the palaces of San Francisco; its long streets lie in regular bars of darkness, east and west, across the sparkling picture; a forest of masts bristles like bulrushes about its feet... . What enchantment of the Arabian Nights can equal this evocation of a roaring city, in a few years of a man's life, from the marshes and the blowing sand. Such swiftness of increase, as with an overgrown youth, suggests a corresponding swiftness of destruction... . Next, perhaps, in order of strangeness to the rapidity of its appearance is the mingling of the races that combine to people it. The town is essentially not Anglo-Saxon; still more essentially not American. The Yankee and the Englishman find themselves alike in a strange country. There are none of those touches - not of nature, and I dare scarcely say of art, - by which the Anglo-Saxon feels himself at home in so great a diversity of lands. Here, on the contrary, are airs of Marseilles and of Pekin. The shops along the streets are like the consulates of different nations. The passers-by vary in features like the slides of a magic lantern.

"Los Angeles? That's just a big parking lot where you buy a hamburger for the trip to San Francisco."
John Lennon

47

Coffee

James Folger was an American businessman, born in New York, who went to San Francisco in the 1850s, lured by the gold rush, but stayed in the city and worked for a company named The Pioneer Steam Coffee and Spice Mills, making coffee. He eventually took over the company in 1872, renaming it after himself. Folger's became one of the largest coffee companies in the United States, and was acquired in 1963 by Proctor & Gamble, who removed the apostrophe from the name.

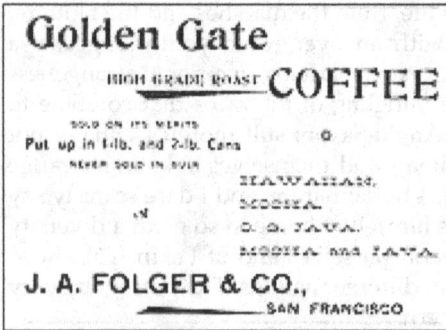

Fancy a novel about Chicago or Buffalo, let us say, or Nashville, Tennessee! There are just three big cities in the United States that are 'story cities' — New York, of course, New Orleans, and, best of the lot, San Francisco.

Frank Norris, author of **McTeague, A Story of San Francisco,** *published in 1899*

Ample And Safe Harborage

This description of San Francisco Bay comes from the book Peculiarities of American Cities *by Willard W. Glazier, published in 1883*

San Francisco Bay is unsurpassed in the world, except by Puget Sound, in Washington Territory, for size, depth, ease of entrance and security. The entrance to the bay is through a passage five miles in length and about two in width, with its shallowest depth about thirty feet at low tide. Rocks rise almost perpendicularly on the northern side of the entrance, to a height of three thousand feet. A lighthouse is placed on one of these, at Point Bonita. Fort Point, a fortress built on solid rock, commands the entrance from the south, and beyond it, until San Francisco is reached, are a series of sand dunes, some of them white and drifting and others showing green with the scant grass growing upon them. The entrance to the bay is called the Golden Gate, a name applied with singular appropriateness, since through its portals have passed continuous streams of gold since the discovery of the latter in 1848. Strangely enough, the name was given before the gold discovery, though at how early a date there seems no means of knowing. As far as can be ascertained, it first appears in Fremont's "Geographical Memoir of California," published in 1847. Six miles eastward from its entrance the bay turns southward for a distance of thirty miles, forming a narrow peninsula between it and the ocean, on the northeastern extremity of which the city is built. It also extends northward to San Puebla Bay, which latter extending eastward, connects by means of a narrow strait with Suisun Bay, into which the Sacramento River discharges its volume of water. These three bays furnish ample and safe harborage for all the merchant fleets of the world.

SAN FRANCISCO AS SEEN FROM MT. TAMALPAIS - MILL VALLEY IN THE FOREGROUND - TIBURON TO THE LEFT - OAKLAND AND BAY CITIES IN THE BACKGROUND - REACHED BY PARLOR CAR TOURS

Isabella Bird

Isabella Bird was arguably the first modern travel writer, traveling widely around the globe through to her death in 1907. Her first book was A Lady's Life in the Rocky Mountains, *published in 1879. In this excerpt, she finds even the memory of San Francisco's urbanity something of a strain. But at least it beats Sacramento.*

It is a weariness to go back, even in thought, to the clang of San Francisco, which I left in its cold morning fog early yesterday, driving to the Oakland ferry through streets with side-walks heaped with thousands of cantaloupe and water-melons, tomatoes, cucumbers, squashes, pears, grapes, peaches, apricots--all of startling size as compared with any I ever saw before. Other streets were piled with sacks of flour, left out all night, owing to the security from rain at this season. I pass hastily over the early part of the journey, the crossing the bay in a fog as chill as November, the number of "lunch baskets," which gave the car the look of conveying a great picnic party, the last view of the Pacific, on which I had looked for nearly a year, the fierce sunshine and brilliant sky inland, the look of long RAINLESSNESS, which one may not call drought, the valleys with sides crimson with the poison oak, the dusty vineyards, with great purple clusters thick among the leaves, and between the vines great dusty melons lying on the dusty earth.

From off the boundless harvest fields the grain was carried in June, and it is now stacked in sacks along the track, awaiting freightage. California is a "land flowing with milk and honey." The barns are bursting with fullness. In the dusty orchards the apple and pear branches are supported, that they may not break down under the weight of fruit; melons, tomatoes, and squashes of gigantic size lie almost unheeded on the ground; fat cattle, gorged almost to repletion, shade themselves under the oaks; superb "red" horses shine, not with grooming, but with condition; and thriving farms everywhere show on what a solid basis the prosperity of the "Golden State" is founded. Very uninviting, however rich, was the blazing Sacramento Valley, and very repulsive the city of Sacramento, which, at a distance of 125 miles from the Pacific, has an elevation of only thirty feet. The mercury stood at 103 degrees in the shade, and the fine white dust was stifling.

> "San Francisco is 49 square miles surrounded by reality."
> *Paul Kantner, a co-founder of the rock band Jefferson Airplane,*
> *one of the groups that re-created the image of San Francisco in the 1960s.*

All The Attractions Of The Next World

In his novel The Picture of Dorian Gray, *published in 1891, the Irish writer Oscar Wilde makes an aptly wry comment on the role of San Francisco in the 19th century as the place to which people looking to escape from other lives fled to start again. Here is an excerpt from the book providing the context to the comment.*

"The people are still discussing poor Basil's disappearance."

"I should have thought they had got tired of that by this time," said Dorian, pouring himself out some wine and frowning slightly.

"My dear boy, they have only been talking about it for six weeks, and the British public are really not equal to the mental strain of having more than one topic every three months. They have been very fortunate lately, however. They have had my own divorce-case and Alan Campbell's suicide. Now they have got the mysterious disappearance of an artist. Scotland Yard still insists that the man in the grey ulster who left for Paris by the midnight train on the ninth of November was poor Basil, and the French police declare that Basil never arrived in Paris at all. I suppose in about a fortnight we shall be told that he has been seen in San Francisco. It is an odd thing, but every one who disappears is said to be seen at San Francisco. It must be a delightful city, and possess all the attractions of the next world."

Oscar Wilde. He would have loved the city in the 1970s

51

"The Chinese Must Go!"

This is an excerpt from the book Peculiarities of American Cities *written by Willard W. Glazier and published in 1883. It takes the "Yellow Peril" approach to the question of Chinese immigration into California.*

There seems to be no assimilation between the Caucasian and the Mongolian on the Pacific slope. In the East an Irish girl recently married a Chinaman; but in San Francisco, though every other race under the sun has united in marriage, the Chinaman is avoided as a pariah. White and yellow races may meet and fraternize in business, in pleasure, and even in crime; but in marriage never. Chinamen rank among the most respected merchants of San Francisco, and these receive exceptional respect as individuals; but between the two races as races a great gulf is fixed. The Chinese immigrant takes no interest in American affairs. His world is on the other side of the Pacific. And the American people return the compliment by taking no interest in him. It is undeniable that, by a certain class of San Francisco citizens, popularly known as Hoodlums, the treatment of the Chinese population has been shameful in the extreme. A Chinaman has no rights which a white man is bound to respect. Insult, contumely, abuse, cruelty and injustice he has been forced to bear at the hands of the rougher classes, without hope of redress. He has been kicked, and cheated, and plundered, and not a voice has been raised in his behalf; but if he has been guilty of the slightest peccadillo, how quickly has he been made to feel the heavy hand of justice!

It seems a pity that before the cry was raised with such overwhelming force, "The Chinese must go!" some little effort had not been made to adapt them to Western civilization. They are quick to take ideas concerning their labor; why not in other things? We have received and adopted the ignorant, vicious hordes from foreign lands to the east of us, and are fast metamorphosing them into intelligent, useful citizens. We are even trying our hand upon the negro, as a late atonement for all the wrong we have done him. But the Indian and the Chinaman seem to be without the pale of our mercy and our Christianity. It might not have been possible, but still the experiment was worth the trying, of attempting to lift them up industrially, educationally and morally, to a level with our own better classes, instead of permitting them to drag us down. Returning to their own country, and carrying back with them our Western civilization, as a little leaven, they might have leavened the whole lump. It is too late for that now, and the mandate has gone forth: "The Chinese must go!" Considering all things as they are, rather than as they might have been, it is undoubtedly better so, and the only salvation of our Pacific States.

An Announcement

Robert Louis Stevenson gives the alternative view on Chinese immigrants in his book, Across the Plains, *published in 1879. The question of what do do about the Chinese was a major political topic in the late 19th century, and in spite of more liberal views such as Stevenson's, the conclusion at the time was basically one of exclusion.*

A while ago it was the Irish, now it is the Chinese that must go. Such is the cry. It seems, after all, that no country is bound to submit to immigration any more than to invasion; each is war to the knife, and resistance to either but legitimate defence. Yet we may regret the free tradition of the republic, which loved to depict herself with open arms, welcoming all unfortunates. And certainly, as a man who believes that he loves freedom, I may be excused some bitterness when I find her sacred name misused in the contention. It was but the other day that I heard a vulgar fellow in the Sand- lot, the popular tribune of San Francisco, roaring for arms and butchery. "At the call of Abraham Lincoln," said the orator, "ye rose in the name of freedom to set free the negroes; can ye not rise and liberate yourselves from a few dirty Mongolians?" For my own part, I could not look but with wonder and respect on the Chinese. Their forefathers watched the stars before mine had begun to keep pigs. Gun-powder and printing, which the other day we imitated, and a school of manners which we never had the delicacy so much as to desire to imitate, were theirs in a long- past antiquity.

Cable Cars

Construction of San Francisco's cable car system began in 1873 and at its height consisted of 23 lines. The advent of electric streetcars had a big impact on the cable cars, and by 1912, only eight cable car lines remained, all operating on routes with steep gradients that the electric streetcars could not handle. Only three are still in operation. Two routes go from the Union Square area to Fisherman's Wharf, and a third route runs along California Street.

The cable cars are powered by a cable running under the street which moves at a constant speed of 9.5mph (15kph), driven from a central power house. The cable cars grab onto the cable to move, or release the grip to stop. The cables are 1.25 inches (3.175 cm) in diameter.

Cable Car on Turn Table at Powell and Market Streets, San Francisco, California

> The cool, grey city of love.
> *George Sterling*

Market at Kearney,
Showing Lotta's
Fountain and
Palace Hotel,
San Francisco,
California 73.

One of San Francisco's best-known landmarks is the Lotta Fountain, now to be found on the corner of Market and Kearney. Prior to 1975, it had been at a nearby location next to the Palace Hotel on Market Street. It was donated to the city in 1875 by Lotta Crabtree, an actress who was the most sought-after star for over 30 years. She retired in 1889 at the age of 42. She was born in New York, but her father moved the family to San Francisco in 1851, and that is where Lotta grew up.

Street Cars Up Houses

Rudyard Kipling in his 1891 best-seller "American Notes," describes the magic of San Francisco's cable cars, able to perform the impossible.

The cable cars have for all practical purposes made San Francisco a dead level. They take no count of rise or fall, but slide equably on their appointed courses from one end to the other of a six-mile street. They turn corners almost at right angles, cross other lines, and for aught I know may run up the sides of houses. There is no visible agency of their flight, but once in awhile you shall pass a five-storied building humming with machinery that winds up an everlasting wire cable, and the initiated will tell you that here is the mechanism. I gave up asking questions. If it pleases Providence to make a car run up and down a slit in the ground for many miles, and if for twopence halfpenny I can ride in that car, why shall I seek the reasons of the miracle? Rather let me look out of the windows till the shops give place to thousands and thousands of little houses made of wood (to imitate stone), each house just big enough for a man and his family. Let me watch the people in the cars and try to find out in what manner they differ from us, their ancestors.

Civil control station during World War II

Night City

San Francisco is essentially a night city, and, next to Paris, I should say it was the gayest night city in the world. . . . The microbe of gaiety . . . is in the air of the place.

> *Maurice Baring*, Round the World in Any Number of Days, *1913.*

Rice Paper

Oscar Wilde, in his lecture entitled Impressions of America, delivered in 1883, had many good things to say about the city, and particularly about its Chinese residents and their customs:

San Francisco is a really beautiful city. China town, peopled by Chinese labourers is the most artistic town I have ever come across. The people, strange melancholy Orientals, whom many people would call common, and they are certainly very poor have deter-mined that they will have nothing about them that is not beautiful. In the Chinese restaurant, where these navvies meet to have supper in the evening, I found them drinking tea out of china cups as delicate as the petals of a rose-leaf, whereas at the gaudy hotels I was supplied with a delf cup an inch and a half thick. When the Chinese bill was presented it was made out on rice paper, the account being done in Indian ink as fantastically as if an artist had been etching little birds on a fan.

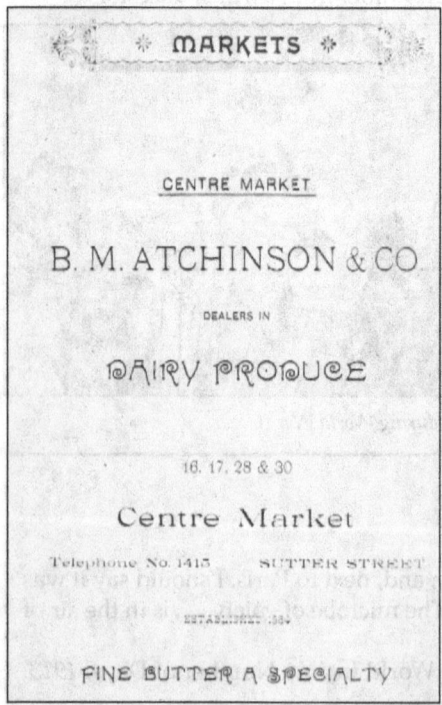
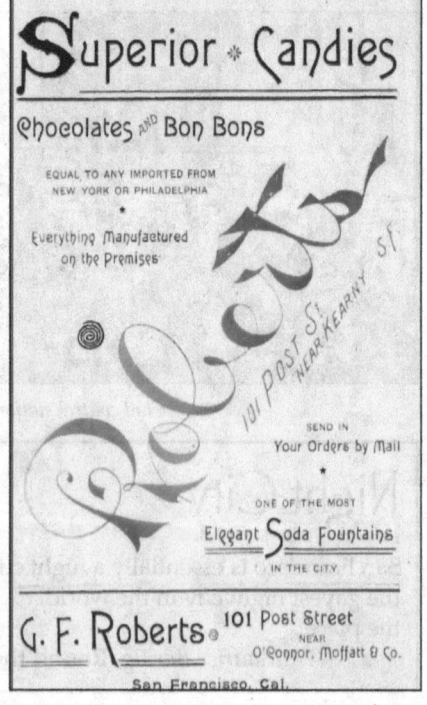

A Mad City

Rudyard Kipling was one the great writers in the English language at the height of the British Empire. In his book American Notes *published in 1891, he included a lively section on San Francisco, where he landed after a long voyage from India. He begins with a quote from the famous 19th century American writer Bret Harte.*

> "Serene, indifferent to fate,
> Thou sittest at the Western Gate;
> Thou sees the white seas fold their tents,
> Oh, warder of two continents;
> Thou drawest all things, small and great,
> To thee, beside the Western Gate."

THIS is what Bret Harte has written of the great city of San Francisco, and for the past fortnight I have been wondering what made him do it. There is neither serenity nor indifference to be found in these parts; and evil would it be for the continents whose wardship were intrusted to so reckless a guardian.

Behold me pitched neck-and-crop from twenty days of the high seas into the whirl of California, deprived of any guidance, and left to draw my own conclusions. Protect me from the wrath of an outraged community if these letters be ever read by American eyes! San Francisco is a mad city--inhabited for the most part by perfectly insane people, whose women are of a remarkable beauty.

When the *City of Pekin* steamed through the Golden Gate, I saw with great joy that the block-house which guarded the mouth of the "finest harbor in the world, sir," could be silenced by two gunboats from Hong Kong with safety, comfort, and despatch. Also, there was not a single American vessel of war in the harbor. This may sound bloodthirsty; but remember, I had come with a grievance upon me--the grievance of the pirated English books.

Oakland Bay Bridge

Dental Parlours

Frank Norris was a successful novelist born in San Francisco whose works included McTeague, *a story set in the city about a dentist who murders his wife. At least two films have been made from the book. This is how it starts:*

It was Sunday, and, according to his custom on that day, McTeague took his dinner at two in the afternoon at the car conductors' coffee-joint on Polk Street. He had a thick gray soup; heavy, underdone meat, very hot, on a cold plate; two kinds of vegetables; and a sort of suet pudding, full of strong butter and sugar. On his way back to his office, one block above, he stopped at Joe Frenna's saloon and bought a pitcher of steam beer. It was his habit to leave the pitcher there on his way to dinner.

Once in his office, or, as he called it on his signboard, "Dental Parlors," he took off his coat and shoes, unbuttoned his vest, and, having crammed his little stove full of coke, lay back in his operating chair at the bay window, reading the paper, drinking his beer, and smoking his huge porcelain pipe while his food digested; crop-full, stupid, and warm. By and by, gorged with steam beer, and overcome by the heat of the room, the cheap tobacco, and the effects of his heavy meal, he dropped off to sleep. Late in the afternoon his canary bird, in its gilt cage just over his head, began to sing. He woke slowly, finished the rest of his beer — very flat and stale by this time — and taking down his concertina from the bookcase, where in week days it kept the company of seven volumes of "Allen's Practical Dentist," played upon it some half-dozen very mournful airs.

McTeague looked forward to these Sunday afternoons as a period of relaxation and enjoyment. He invariably spent them in the same fashion. These were his only pleasures — to eat, to smoke, to sleep, and to play upon his concertina.

The six lugubrious airs that he knew, always carried him back to the time when he was a car-boy at the Big Dipper Mine in Placer County, ten years before. He remembered the years he had spent there trundling the heavy cars of ore in and out of the tunnel under the direction of his father. For thirteen days of each fortnight his father was a steady, hard-working shift-boss of the mine. Every other Sunday he became an irresponsible animal, a beast, a brute, crazy with alcohol.

McTeague remembered his mother, too, who, with the help of the Chinaman, cooked for forty miners. She was an overworked drudge, fiery and energetic for all that, filled with the one idea of having her son rise in life and enter a profession. The chance had come at last when the father died, corroded with alcohol, collapsing in a few hours. Two or three years later a travelling dentist visited the mine and put up his tent near the bunk-house. He was more or less of a charlatan, but he fired Mrs. McTeague's ambition, and young McTeague went away with him to learn his profession. He had learnt it after a fashion, mostly by watching the charlatan operate. He had read many of the necessary books, but he was too hopelessly stupid to get much benefit from them.

Then one day at San Francisco had come the news of his mother's death; she had left him some money — not much, but enough to set him up in business; so he had cut loose from the charlatan and had opened his "Dental Parlors" on Polk Street, an "accommodation street" of small shops in the residence quarter of the town. Here he had slowly collected a clientele of butcher boys, shop girls, drug clerks, and car conductors. He made but few acquaintances. Polk Street called him the "Doctor" and spoke of his enormous strength. For McTeague was a young giant, carrying his huge shock of blond hair six feet three inches from the ground; moving his immense limbs, heavy with ropes of muscle, slowly, ponderously. His hands were enormous, red, and covered with a fell of stiff yellow hair; they were hard as wooden mallets, strong as vises, the hands of the old-time car-boy. Often he dispensed with forceps and extracted a refractory tooth with his thumb and finger. His head was square-cut, angular; the jaw salient, like that of the carnivora.

McTeague's mind was as his body, heavy, slow to act, sluggish. Yet there was nothing vicious about the man. Altogether he suggested the draught horse, immensely strong, stupid, docile, obedient.

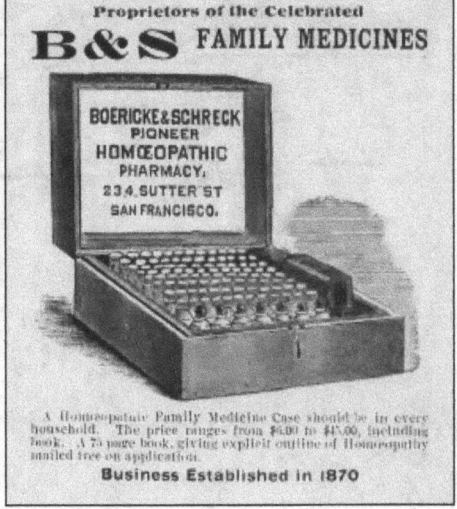

An Ugly Brute

H.G. Wells wrote many wonderful stories, but The Island of Doctor Moreau *is one of the most bizarre, following Englishman Edward Prendick, a shipwrecked sailor who visits the home of Doctor Moreau. He finds Moreau performing diabolic experiments, creating human-like beings from animals using vivisection. San Francisco comes into the story as the place where one of the creatures was allegedly brought from, no doubt shanghai-ed.*

"Montgomery," said I, suddenly, as the outer door closed, "why has your man pointed ears?"

"Damn!" he said, over his first mouthful of food. He stared at me for a moment, and then repeated, "Pointed ears?"

"Little points to them," said I, as calmly as possible, with a catch in my breath; "and a fine black fur at the edges?"

He helped himself to whiskey and water with great deliberation. "I was under the impression that his hair covered his ears."

"I saw them as he stooped by me to put that coffee you sent to me on the table. And his eyes shine in the dark."

By this time Montgomery had recovered from the surprise of my question. "I always thought," he said deliberately, with a certain accentuation of his flavouring of lisp, "that there was something the matter with his ears, from the way he covered them. What were they like?"

I was persuaded from his manner that this ignorance was a pretence. Still, I could hardly tell the man that I thought him a liar. "Pointed," I said; "rather small and furry,--distinctly furry. But the whole man is one of the strangest beings I ever set eyes on."

A sharp, hoarse cry of animal pain came from the enclosure behind us. Its depth and volume testified to the puma. I saw Montgomery wince.

"Yes?" he said.

"Where did you pick up the creature?"

"San Francisco. He's an ugly brute, I admit. Half-witted, you know. Can't remember where he came from. But I'm used to him, you know. We both are. How does he strike you?"

"He's unnatural," I said. "There's something about him—don't think me fanciful, but it gives me a nasty little sensation, a tightening of my muscles, when he comes near me. It's a touch of the diabolical, in fact."

San Francisco harbor, circa 1851

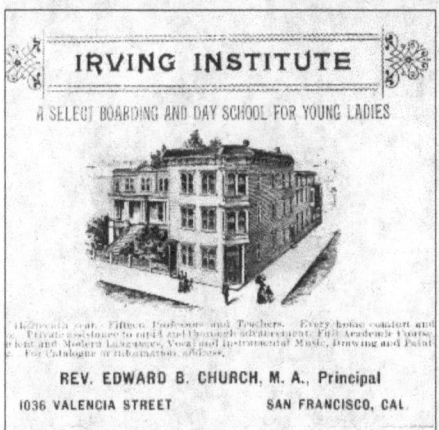

IRVING INSTITUTE

A SELECT BOARDING AND DAY SCHOOL FOR YOUNG LADIES

REV. EDWARD B. CHURCH, M. A., Principal

1036 VALENCIA STREET   SAN FRANCISCO, CAL.

"I'd rather be a busted lamp post on Battery Street, San Francisco, than the Waldorf-Astoria."

This quote is attributed to Willie Britt in a newspaper article published in the San Francisco newspaper The Sun *on April 21, 1906, just three days after the great earthquake and fire which destroyed much of the original town.*

Investigations into the identity of Willie Britt have been fruitless, but he had a neat turn of phrase

Refinement of Manner

Oscar Wilde had a way with words and a unique eye for seeing contrasts and anomalies. In a lecture he gave on the topic of House Decoration during a tour of the United States in 1882. In it, he used a story about San Francisco Chinatown to illustrate his point, that there is more honor in making things than selling them.

We should see more of the workman than we do. We should not be content to have the salesman stand between us - the salesman who knows nothing of what he is selling save that he is charging a great deal too much for it. And watching the workman will teach that most important lesson - the nobility of all rational workmanship. I said in my last lecture that art would create a new brotherhood among men by furnishing a universal language. I said that under its beneficent influences war might pass away. Thinking this, what place can I ascribe to art in our education? If children grow up among all fair and lovely things, they will grow to love beauty and detest ugliness before they know the reason why. If you go into a house where everything is coarse, you find things chipped and broken and unsightly. Nobody exercises any care. If everything is dainty and delicate, gentleness and refinement of manner are unconsciously acquired. When I was in San Francisco I used to visit the Chinese Quarter

frequently. There I used to watch a great hulking Chinese workman at his task of digging, and used to see him every day drink his tea from a little cup as delicate in texture as the petal of a flower, whereas in all the grand hotels of the land, where thousands of dollars have been lavished on great gilt mirrors and gaudy columns, I have been given my coffee or my chocolate in cups an inch and a quarter thick. I think I have deserved something nicer.

San Francisco is a mad city inhabited for the most part by perfectly insane people whose women are of remarkable beauty.
Rudyard Kipling, From Sea to Sea, *1889.*

Five women dressed in traditional Chinese clothing read the day's headlines

Chinatown 1900

Arnold Genthe was a photographer born in Germany in 1869 who is most famous for his wonderful photographs of San Francisco Chinatown around the year 1900, revealing the resilience of Chinese culture in the enclave even in the new land of America. Here are three of his Chinatown images:

> What fetched me instantly (and thousands of other newcomers with me) was the subtle but unmistakable sense of escape from the United States.
> H.L. Mencken, a writer born in 1880 and known as "the Sage of Baltimore."

A taproom in San Francisco, 1904

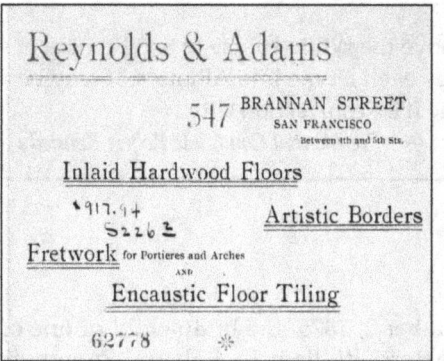
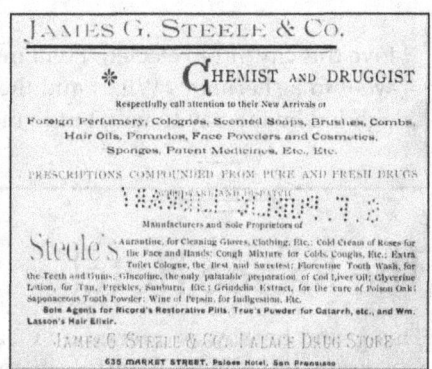
Fancy a novel about Chicago or Buffalo, let us say, or Nashville, Tennessee! There are just three big cities in the United States that are 'story cities'— New York, of course, New Orleans, and, best of the lot, San Francisco.

Frank Norris, author (1870-1902)

HUNDREDS OF THOUSANDS OF WILD DUCK HAUNT THE MARSHY SHORELINE OF SOME PARTS OF SAN FRANCISCO BAY, AFFORDING THE FINEST SPORT DURING THE SEASON

Promotional postcard for duck-hunting in San Francisco, 1915

I love this city. If I'm elected, I will move the White House to San Francisco. I went to Fisherman's Wharf and they even let me into Allioto`s. It may be Baghdad by the Bay to you, but to me it's Resurrection City.

Presidential Candidate Robert Kennedy

The Palace Hotel

This grand hotel was opened on October 2, 1875, the brain child of one of San Francisco's most colorful characters, William C. Ralston, known as the "Magician of San Francisco". By the opening, however, his magic had failed, and he was dead, possibly a suicide. His body was found floating in the Bay. He built the Palace Hotel on the southwest corner of Market and Montgomery. It took four years to build and was considered the most magnificent structure west of the Rockies. It was known as "Bonanza Inn", and for three roaring decades played a central and elegant role in the life of San Francisco. It had seven stories and a central Grand Court. It had 755

guest rooms each with a private bathroom.

Then at 5:12 A.M. on Wednesday, April 18, 1906, the earthquake struck. The Palace Hotel survived the shock, but later that day, the fires that broke out around the city touched the hotel and in a short time the hotel was reduced to a smoldering shell.

In December 1909, just forty-three months after the death of the original Palace, a "new" Palace opened with nine floors rather than seven. It is still in business. Dinner in the Palm Court, drinks at the "Pied Piper" Bar.

> "San Francisco is a city where people are never more abroad than when they are at home."
> *Benjamin F. Taylor*

> "God took the beauty of the Bay of Naples, the Valley of the Nile, the Swiss Alps, the Hudson River Valley, rolled them into one and made San Francisco Bay."
> *Fiorello La Guardia*

A Vast Marble-Paved Hall

Rudyard Kipling in his 1891 best-seller "American Notes," describes the hotel in which he stayed while in San Francisco, the Palace Hotel, which is still in business on the corner of Market and New Montgomery streets.

There were no more incidents till I reached the Palace Hotel, a seven-storied warren of humanity with a thousand rooms in it. All the travel books will tell you about hotel arrangements in this country. They should be seen to be appreciated. Understand clearly — and this letter is written after a thousand miles of experiences — that money will not buy you service in the West. When the hotel clerk — the man who awards your room to you and who is supposed to give you information — when that resplendent individual stoops to attend to your wants he does so whistling or hum-ming or picking his teeth, or pauses to converse with some one he knows. These performances, I gather, are to impress upon you that he is a free man and your equal. From his general appearance

It's part San Francisco. A bit of England. The flavor of New York

The earthquake of April 18, 1906 also caused fires in many parts of the city, and one casualty was the grand and famous Palace Hotel

and the size of his diamonds he ought to be your superior. There is no necessity for this swaggering self-consciousness of freedom. Business is business, and the man who is paid to attend to a man might reasonably devote his whole attention to the job. Out of office hours he can take his coach and four and pervade society if he pleases.

In a vast marble-paved hall, under the glare of an electric light, sat forty or fifty men, and for their use and amusement were provided spittoons of infinite capacity and generous gape. Most of the men wore frock-coats and top-hats—the things that we in India put on at a wedding-breakfast, if we possess them—but they all spat. They spat on principle. The spittoons were on the staircases, in each bedroom—yea, and in chambers even more sacred than these. They chased one into retirement, but they blossomed in chiefest splendor round the bar, and they were all used, every reeking one of them.

The Caselli Mansion

The Caselli Mansion at 250 Douglass Street in the Castro district of San Francisco was built by a colorful gentleman named Alfred E. Clarke and completed in 1896. Clarke served for a number as clear to the Chief of Police, and made a fortune on the side running a loan operation. The house survived the earthquake in 1906 and is now a city monument.

Spiritually Lacking?

"It is hardly fair to blame America for the state of San Francisco, for its population is cosmopolitan and its seaport attracts the floating vice of the Pacific; but be the cause what it may, there is much room for spiritual betterment."

Sir Arthur Conan Doyle, author of the Sherlock Holmes stories

They say that in San Francisco there is less than meets the eye:
in Los Angeles there is far more.
Travel writer Jan Morris, Destinations, *1980.*

Maidens Of Generous Build

*In this excerpt from his 1891 best-seller "American Notes", Rudyard Kipling
discusses the women he observed on the streets of San Francisco.*

Night fell over the Pacific, and the white sea-fog whipped through the streets,
dimming the splendors of the electric lights. It is the use of this city, her men
and women folk, to parade between the hours of eight and ten a certain street
called Cairn Street, where the finest shops are situated. Here the click of high
heels on the pavement is loudest, here the lights are brightest, and here the
thunder of the traffic is most overwhelming. I watched Young California, and
saw that it was, at least, expensively dressed, cheerful in manner, and self-
asserting in conversation. Also the women were very fair. Perhaps eighteen
days aboard ship had something to do with my unreserved admiration. The
maidens were of generous build, large, well groomed, and attired in raiment
that even to my inexperienced eyes must have cost much. Cairn Street at nine
o'clock levels all distinctions of rank as impartially as the grave. Again and
again I loitered at the heels of a couple of resplendent beings, only to overhear,
when I expected the level voice of culture, the staccato "Sez he," "Sez I" that is
the mark of the white servant-girl all the world over.

2074 — PALACE HOTEL (AND LOTTA'S FOUNTAIN), SAN FRANCISCO, CALIFORNIA

SING FAT CO., INC.
THE FAMOUS ORIENTAL BAZAAR
S.W. CORNER CALIFORNIA ST. AND GRANT AVE.,
CHINATOWN.
SAN FRANCISCO, CALIFORNIA.
BRANCH: 548-550 SOUTH BROADWAY,
LOS ANGELES.
司公發生埠正山金國美

Mid-Winter's Fair 1894

In 1894, the California economy was in pretty bad shape, and the example of a large and successful exposition in Chicago the previous year encouraged San Franciscans to try something similar. A large area of Golden Gate Park has turned over to the event and large buildings erected to attract visitors. Exhibits included a Japanese tea house, a Mechanical Arts Exhibition - machinery was a big deal at the end of the 19th century - and a small Ferris Wheel - the Chicago event had featured the first-ever Ferris wheel and had been a sensation.

78

Panama-Pacific Exposition 1915

San Francisco organized an exposition in 1915, much grander and larger in scale than the event in 1894. A key attraction was the Tower of Jewels. Lit here by spotlights.

From Robert Louis Stevenson's memoir, Across the Plains, *published in 1879.*

By afternoon we were at Sacramento, the city of gardens in a plain of corn; and the next day before the dawn we were lying to upon the Oakland side of San Francisco Bay. The day was breaking as we crossed the ferry; the fog was rising over the citied hills of San Francisco; the bay was perfect - not a ripple, scarce a stain, upon its blue expanse; everything was waiting, breathless, for the sun. A spot of cloudy gold lit first upon the head of Tamalpais, and then widened downward on its shapely shoulder; the air seemed to awaken, and began to sparkle; and suddenly "The tall hills Titan discovered,"and the city of San Francisco, and the bay of gold and corn, were lit from end to end with summer daylight.

The Spirit of the West

*The 1915 Panama-Pacigfic Exposition was a huge event for
San Francisco. A handbook was published describing the
many buildings constructed for the event, written by Juliet
James. Here is her foreword, entitled "The Pastel City by
the Sea."*

There is a hill-crowned city by a silver sea, near a
Golden Gate. For ages the water has washed from an
almost land-locked bay against this hill-crowned city,
and on its northern side has created of the shore an
amphitheatre stretching for some three miles to the
western headlands.

Behind this amphitheatre rises, in terraces, the steep
hills of this water-lashed city, and in part, a forest of
pines stretches to the west. Man has flanked this reach
of shore by two lowering forts, and in front, across the
sapphire sea, one looks onto the long undulations of
hills, climaxed by grand old Tamalpais.

Just three years ago and one saw in this same low-lying shore only a marshy
stretch, with lagoons working their way far into the land - the home of the seagull.

There came a time when, had you looked closely, you would have seen coming
thru the Golden Gate a phantom flotilla of caravels, freighted with clever ideas.

On the vessels came; at the prows were several noble figures: Energy,
Enterprise, Youth, the Spirit of the East, the Spirit of the West,
Success, and in the last caravel, the stalwart Mother of Tomorrow.

They had dug and delved with mighty Hercules and had created that great gap
that has severed two continents. Then, leaving their work to be finished, they had
sailed on to celebrate their triumph in the Land of El Dorado, the region of their
desires.

In a shallop in front of these floating winged vessels, riding on the waves, came
Venus, rowed by the fairies - in her hand the golden ball of opportunity.

The mermaids, the dolphins, the little sea-horses sported in the wake of these
vessels, leaving a long line of foam and silver as they sped on.

Over the waves they came to the Golden Land of the Pacific. They moored their
vessels by the fort-flanked shores, and stepping out upon the haunt of the seagull,
they moved boldly across this unsightly stretch of wave-washed land.

Enterprise and Energy pushed ahead: the Fairy ever flitting near. At a signal
from Enterprise the Fairy turned her wheel, Venus threw her golden ball of

opportunity, and lo! out of the foam of the sea rose a Venus city with the round sea bubbles resting on the roofs.

One day a man appeared on the hilltop o'erlooking this wondrous city and by his magic power, being filled with music, with color-music, he cast a spell and behold a pastel city by the sea - such an one as only those who dream could think of; a city glowing with warmth of color, with a softness and mystical charm such as only the brain of Jules Guerin could produce.

He is the conductor of this wondrous symphony, this beautiful Mozart fantasia, and if you listen, you can hear the strains of the great beautiful melodies wafted now east, now west, now north, now south, rising to great climaxes, falling back to great chords of harmony, or, in an allegro movement, causing you almost to trip with delight in the joy of it all.

Your eye is enthralled with the beauty of the coloring. One sees turquoise green domes floating in a silver-moated ether, long colonnades of glacial ice columns leading to regions beyond, where quiet silver pools throw back the mirrored glories.

Battalions of daffodils holding their long sabers stand in the South Garden, making ready for the great festival. Soon those daffodils will raise their golden trumpets and will sound the fanfare at the opening of the Great Jubilee, and up will spring two hundred thousand wide-eyed yellow pansies to look and wonder at the marvelous beauty and help in the hallelujah chorus that will be one great poeon of joy - one splendid hymn of praise.

And the blue eucalypti against the walls will lend their voices, the yellow acacias will add their cadences; while down by the great lagoon, ten thousand periwinkles will dance for joy.

Far out on the waters will be intoned to the rhythm of the waves a chorus from white-robed water-lilies, who, like a throng of choristers, will send their anthems rippling over the sun-kissed waves.

The Spirit of the East that has added its domes, its minarets, its soft-glowing colors, will remain and join hands with the Spirit of the West, that strong, pulsating energetic spirit, and the harmony produced will vibrate from the shores of the Occident to the shores of the Orient and bring about a better understanding, a great world peace.

And the world will come to listen. The great music will sound across the waters, and the world will be the better in its way of thinking, of working, of living - and all because of the great beauty. Wonderful is it to be living today, to have the opportunity of watching the beginning of this mighty growth; to be present at one of the world's greatest events.

And the pastel city by the sea will not leave us, for, as the years go on, whatever be our mission, the vision of this dream-city will float before us, leading us to finer, higher works, strengthening our ideals, and causing us to give only of our finest fiber.

In China Town

A description of an excursion into the "alien" world of San Francisco Chinatown from the book Byways Around San Francisco Bay *by W. E. Hutchinson, published in 1915.*

If you are a tourist, making your first visit to San Francisco, you will inquire at once for Chinatown, the settlement of the Celestial Kingdom, dropped down, as it were, in the very heart of a big city; a locality where you are as far removed from anything American as if you were in Hongkong or Foochow. Chinatown is only about two blocks wide by eight blocks long; yet in this small area from ten to fifteen thousand Chinese live, and cling with all the tenacity of the race to their Oriental customs and native dress. They are as clean as a new pin about their person, but how they can keep so immaculate amid such careless and not over-clean surroundings is a mystery not to be solved by a white man.

For a few dollars a guide will conduct a party through Chinatown, and point out all the places of interest; but we preferred to act for ourselves in this capacity, and saunter from place to place as our fancy dictated. Stores of all kinds line both sides of Grant Avenue, formerly called Dupont, where all kinds of Chinese merchandise are displayed in profusion. At one place we stopped to examine some most exquisite ivory carvings, as delicate in tracery as frost on a window pane. Next we lingered before a shop where the women of our party went into raptures over the exquisite gowns and the beautiful needlework displayed. Here are shown padded silks of the most delicate shades, on which deft fingers have embroidered the ever-present Chinese stork and cherry blossoms, as realistic as if painted with an artist's brush.

That peculiar building just across the way is the Kow Nan Low Restaurant, resplendent with dragons and lanterns of every shape and size suspended above and about the doorway.

If you are fond of chop suey, or bird's-nest pudding, and are not too fastidious as to its ingredients, you may enjoy a dinner fit for a mandarin.

We stop before a barber shop and watch the queer process of shaving the head and braiding the queue. The barber does not invite inspection, as the curtains are partly drawn, but we peep over the top and look with interest at the queer process of tonsorial achievement, much to the disgust of the barber and his customer, if the expression on their faces can be taken as an index of their thoughts.

Then to the drug store, the market, the shoeshop, and a dozen other places, to finally bring up where all the tourists do—at the "Marshall Field's" of Chinatown, Sing Fat's, a truly marvelous place, where one can spend hours looking over the countless objects of interest.

One of the pleasures of Chinatown is to see the children of rich and poor on the street, dressed in their Oriental costumes, looking like tiny yellow flowers, as they pick their way daintily along the walk, or are carried in the arms of the happy father—never the mother. If you would make the father smile, show an interest in the boy he is carrying so proudly.

To gamble is a Chinaman's second nature. Games of fan-tan and pie-gow are constantly in operation; and the police either tolerate or are powerless to stop them. Tong wars are of frequent occurrence, crime and its punishment being so mixed up that an outsider cannot unravel them. The San Francisco police have struggled with the question, but have finally left the Chinese to settle their own affairs after their own fashion. Opium dens flourish as a matter of course, for opium and Chinese are synonymous words. You can tell an opium fiend as far as you can see him; his face looks like wet parchment stretched over a skull and dried, making a truly gruesome sight. Every ship that comes into the bay from the Orient is searched for opium, and quantities of it are found hidden away under the planking, or in other places less likely to be detected by the sharp-eyed officials. When found it is at once confiscated.

The Chinese are an extremely superstitious people, and it is very difficult to get a photograph of them, for they flee from the camera man as from the wrath to come. When you think you are about to get a good picture, and are ready to press the button, he either covers his face, or turns his back to you. The writer was congratulating himself on the picture he was about to take of four Chinese women in their native costumes, and was just going to make the exposure, when four Chinamen who were watching him deliberately stepped in front of the camera, completely spoiling the negative. The younger generation, and especially the girls, will occasionally pose for you, and a truly picturesque group they make in their queer mannish dress of bright colors, as they laugh and chatter in their odd but musical jargon.

A few years ago you could not persuade a Chinaman to talk into a telephone, for, as one of them said, "No can see talkee him," meaning he could not see the speaker. Another said, "Debil talkee, me no likee him," but now this is all changed. Some there are who still cling to their old superstitions, but they are few. The march of commerce levels all prejudices, and the telephone is an established fact in Chinatown. They have their own exchange, a small building built in Chinese style, and their own operators. Even the San Francisco telephone book has one section devoted to them, and printed in Chinese characters. And so civilization goes marching on the old order changeth, and even the Chinaman must of necessity conform to our ways.

But the Chinatown of to-day is not the Chinatown existent before the great disaster of 1906. It has changed, and that for the better, better both for the city and the Chinaman.

Mr. Arnold Genthe, in his Old Chinatown, says: "I think we first glimpsed the real man through our gradual understanding of his honesty. American merchants learned that none need ever ask a note of a Chinaman in any commercial transaction; his word was his bond." And while they still have their joss houses, worship their idols, gamble, and smoke opium, they are their own worst enemies; they do not bother the white men, and are generally considered a law unto themselves.

As we pass on down Grant Avenue we meet a crowd gathered around a bulletin board, where hundreds of red and yellow posters are displayed. All are excited, chattering like magpies, as they discuss the latest bulletin of a Tong war, or some other notice of equal interest; and here we leave them, and Chinatown also, passing over the line out of the precincts of the Celestial, and into our own "God's country."

Chinatown San Francisco, ca. 1900. Before fire and earthquake. By Arnold Genthe

A CHINESE MEAT AND VEGETABLE MARKET, CHINATOWN, SAN FRANCISCO, CAL.

549. Chinese Joss House, Chinatown,
San Francisco, Cal.

548. Market Scene in Chinatown,
San Francisco, Cal.

Selected Locations

Civic Center - laid out immediately after the 1906 earthquake destroyed the original City Hall.

City Hall - designed by Arthur Brown Jr, and opened in 1915, it features the fifth largest dome in the world, 42 feet taller than that of the US Congress in Washington DC.

Bill Graham Civic Auditorium - Opened in 1915 as part of the 1915 Panama-Pacific International Expo, and currently named after the rock concert promoter of the 1960s and 1970s.

War Memorial Veteran's Building - Built for the 1915 Panama-Pacific Expo. The United Nations charter was signed here in 1951, as well as the 1951 peace treaty between Japan and the United States.

San Francisco Armory, corner of Mission Street and 14th - Opened in 1914 to replace a structure destroyed in the 1906 earthquake. It served as the local headquarters of the National Guard for many years and was the control point for the suppression of the 1934 general strike.

The top of page one of The Morning Call, *April 2, 1890*

A Diction of Solecisms

The Devil's Dictionary, *written by Ambrose Bierce and published in 1906, has an entry that mentions San Francisco as follows:*

SANDLOTTER, n. A vertebrate mammal holding the political views of Denis Kearney, a notorious demagogue of San Francisco, whose audiences gathered in the open spaces (sandlots) of the town. True to the traditions of his species, this leader of the proletariat was finally bought off by his law-and-order enemies, living prosperously silent and dying impenitently rich. But before his treason he imposed upon California a constitution that was a confection of sin in a diction of solecisms. The similarity between the words "sandlotter" and "sansculotte" is problematically significant, but indubitably suggestive.

Newspaper stand at Kearny and Sutter, 1941

1906 San Francisco Earthquake

The San Francisco earthquake struck at 5.12am on April 18, 1906 and the main tremor lasted for 42 seconds. Huge fires broke out all over the city as a result of the rupture, which would have registered around 7.8 on the Richter scale, and about 3,000 people died. More than 80 percent of the city was destroyed. Some experts believe the hydraulic mining used in the later years of the gold rush triggered the quake. It was one of the worst natural disasters in US history.

505. Market Street, looking East from Powell St., San Francisco, Cal

By the time of this postcard circa 1920s, San Francisco had been fully rebuilt after the earthquake

The ruins of The Palace Hotel, Monadnock Building, and Call Building soon after the April 18, 1906 earthquake, which resulted in devastating fires in many parts of the city

> I'm just mad for San Francisco. It is like London and Paris stacked on top of each other.
> *Twiggy, and English model, super-hot in the late 1960s.*

The Nether Regions

By 1906, the year of San Francisco's devastating earthquake, Mark Twain was 71 years of age and the grand old man of American letters. Soon after the earthquake, he was asked for his view of the event by reporters who attended a speech he had given. Here is what he said:

I haven't been there since 1868, and that great city of San Francisco has grown up since my day. When I was there she had one hundred and eighteen thousand people, and of this number eighteen thousand were Chinese. I was a reporter on the Virginia City Enterprise in Nevada in 1862, and stayed there, I think, about two years, when I went to San Francisco and got a job as a reporter on *The Call*. I was there three or four years.

I remember one day I was walking down Third Street in San Francisco. It was a sleepy, dull Sunday afternoon, and no one was stirring. Suddenly as I looked up the street about three hundred yards the whole side of a house fell out. The street was full of bricks and mortar. At the same time I was knocked against the side of a house and stood there stunned for a moment.

I thought it was an earthquake. Nobody else had heard anything about it and no one said earthquake to me afterward, but I saw it and I wrote it. Nobody else wrote it, and the house I saw go into the street was the only house in the city that felt it. I've always wondered if it wasn't a little performance gotten up for my especial entertainment by the nether regions.

At the end of the trail stands the historic new Palace Hotel, San Francisco

A detail of the letterhead paper used by the Palace Hotel in San Francisco in the 1920s, with an "End of the Trail" theme. Many of San Francisco's residents in the late 19th century had made it to the city during the gold rush in such a manner

FLEE IN PANIC
FROM PALACE,
SAYS WITNESS

Egbert H. Gould, president of the Chicago Car Heating company of Chicago, reached Los Angeles yesterday morning at 11 o'clock. He was present in San Francisco during all the horrors of the first shocks.

"The first shock threw me from my bed halfway across the floor of my room in the sixth story of the Palace hotel. Realizing what was occuring and fearing a collapse of the building I rushed down to the main corridor on the ground floor of the hotel.

"I was the first person to reach the office of the hostelry. The employes and clerks were running about like madmen. Quickly men, women and children filled the office. There they stood with faces blanched, held by a spell of awe.

"Hastily I rushed back to my room where I secured my clothing. Attired in my pajamas I made my way to the Western Union telegraph office to wire my wife in Los Angeles. The telegraphers were at their stations and seemed to be the only cool persons in the whole city.

"Amid the shower of falling bricks and stones and rain of shattered glass I sat on the curbing and picked from the soles of my feet pieces of broken glass. Then I dressed there in the street, but in the short time the buildings within three blocks below the Palace had broken out into flames. Billows of flames were sweeping up the business district.

"As I passed the Call building at Third and Market streets I noticed that it was more than a foot out of plumb, and was hanging over the street like the tower of Pisa. I remained in San Francisco until 7 o'clock and then took the ferry to Oakland. However, I returned about two hours later.

"When I attempted to get passage on the Oakland ferry about 11 o'clock people were fighting like madmen to get aboard the boat. Many were nearly transfixed in their efforts to climb over the iron gates. Everyone seemed devoid of reason and their only thought was to get away.

"Like a tidal wave the people flooded on the ferry boat and had I not been a strong man I would have been severely injured—perhaps killed. I got to Oakland safely and left at 5 o'clock for Los Angeles."

"San Francisco is poetry. Even the hills rhyme."

Pat Montandon, described as being "an American author, California socialite, and humanitarian." She moved to San Francisco in 1960 and became known as Party Girl Pat, famous for throwing the most fabulous parties in the city.

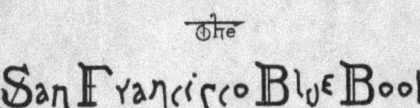

the
San Francisco Blue Book

BEING THE

FASHIONABLE PRIVATE ADDRESS DIRECTORY AND
LADIES' VISITING AND SHOPPING GUIDE

Containing the Names, Addresses, Reception Days and Country
Residences of the Elite of San Francisco, Oakland,
Alameda, Los Angeles, Menlo Park, Redwood City,
San Mateo, Sacramento, San Diego, San
Jose and Santa Clara, San Rafael,
Sausalito, Stockton, and
California Colony in
New York

SEASON 1889-90

SAN FRANCISCO
THE BANCROFT COMPANY
1889

Cliff House

There have been five incarnatioins of Cliff House on the Pacific coast on the western edge of San Francisco peninsula. The most picturesque version was built in 1897 and survived the 1906 earthquake only to be destroyed in a fire in September 1907. The latest version is famous for its breakfasts, as well as its ocean views.

The City That Was

The Sun, *a San Francisco newspaper, published a long and moving tribute to the old city on April 21, 1906, just days after it had been largely destroyed by earthqiuake and flames. The author was Will Urwin, and it was subtitled* "A Requiem of Old San Francisco." *Here are some excerpts:*

The old San Francisco is dead. The gayest, lightest hearted, most pleasure loving city of the western continent, and in many ways the most interesting and romantic, is a horde of refugees living among ruins. It may rebuild; it probably will; but those who have known that peculiar city by the Golden Gate, have caught its flavor of the Arabian Nights, feel that it can never be the same. It is as though a pretty, frivolous woman had passed through a great tragedy. She survives, but she is sobered and different. If it rises out of the ashes it must be a modern city, much like other cities and without its old atmosphere....

The externals of the city are--or were, for they are no more--just as curious. One usually entered San Francisco by way of the Bay. Across its yellow flood, covered with the fleets from the strange seas of the Pacific,San Francisco presented itself in a hill panorama. Probably no other city of the world, excepting perhaps Naples, could be so viewed at first sight. It rose above the passenger, as he reached dockage, in a succession of hill terraces. At one side was Telegraph Hill, the end of the peninsula, a height so abrupt that it had a one hundred and fifty foot sheer cliff on its seaward frontage. Further along lay Nob Hill, crowned with the Mark Hopkins mansion, which had the effect of a citadel, and in later years by the great, white Fairmount. Further along was Russian Hill, the highest point. Below was the business district, whose low site caused all the trouble.

Except for the modern buildings, the fruit of the last ten years, the town presented at first sight a disreputable appearance. Most of the buildings were low and of wood. In the middle period of the '70's, when, a great part of San Francisco was building, the newly-rich perpetrated some atrocious architecture. In that time, too every one put bow windows on his house to catch all of the morning sunlight that was coming through the fog; and those little houses, with bow windows and fancy work all down their fronts, were characteristic of the middle class residence districts. Then the Italians, who tumbled over Telegraph Hill, had built as they listed and with little regard for streets, and their houses hung crazily on a side hill which was little less than a precipice. The Chinese, although they occupied an abandoned business district, had remade their dwellings Chinese fashion, and the Mexicans and Spaniards had added to their houses those little balconies without which life is not life to a Spaniard....

And it was a city of romance and a gateway to adventure. It opened out on the mysterious Pacific, the untamed ocean; and through the Golden Gate entered China, Japan, the South Sea Islands, Lower California, the west coast of Central America, Australia. There was a sprinkling, too, of Alaska and Siberia. From his windows on Russian Hill one saw always something strange and suggestive creeping through the mists of the bay. It would be a South Sea Island brig, bringing in copra, to take out cottons and idols; a Chinese junk after sharks' livers; an old whaler, which seemed to drip oil, home from a year of cruising in the Arctic. Even the tramp windjammers were deep-chested craft, capable of rounding the Horn or of circumnavigating the globe; and they came in streaked and picturesque from their long voyaging. In the orange colored dawn which always comes through the mists of that bay, the fishing fleet would crawl in under triangular lateen sails; for the fishermen of San Francisco Bay are all Neapolitans who have brought their customs and sail with lateen rigs stained an orange brown and shaped, when the wind fills them, like the ear of a horse. Along the waterfront the people of these craft met. "The smelting pot of the races," Stevenson called it; and this was always the city of his soul. There were black Gilbert Islanders, almost indistinguishable from negroes; lighter Kanakas from Hawaii or Samoa; Lascars in turbans; thickset Russian sailors, wild Chinese with unbraided hair; Italian fishermen in tam o' shanters, loud shirts and blue sashes; Greeks, Alaska Indians, little bay Spanish-Americans, together with men of all the European races. These came in and out from among the queer craft, to lose themselves in the disreputable, tumble-down, but always mysterious shanties and small saloons. In the back rooms of these saloons
South Sea Island traders and captains, fresh from the lands of romance, whaling masters, people who were trying to get up treasure expeditions, filibusters, Alaskan miners, used to meet and trade adventures.

There was another element, less picturesque and equally characteristic, along the waterfront. San Francisco was the back eddy of European civilization--one end of the world. The drifters came there and stopped, lingered a while to live by their wits in a country where living after a fashion has always been marvellously cheap. These people haunted the waterfront and the Barbary Coast by night, and lay by day on the grass in Portsmouth Square....

The Barbary Coast was a loud bit of hell. No one knows who coined the name. The place was simply three blocks of solid dance halls, there for the delight of the sailors of the world. On a fine busy night every door blared loud dance music from orchestras, steam pianos and gramaphones, and the cumulative effect of the sound which reached the street was chaos and pandemonium. Almost anything might be happening behind the swinging doors....

The Palace Hotel was destroyed in the earthquake and fires of 1906, but it was rebuilt and re-opened. This is an advertisement for the hotel from 1911

97

Fairmont Hotel

This luxury hostelry on top of Nob Hill was under construction when the earthquake struck in 1906, but its structure survived, and the hotel opened in 1907. It was named after mining magnate and U.S. Senator James Graham Fair.

THE FAIRMONT HOTEL · ATOP NOB HILL · SAN FRANCISCO

Octagon Houses were popular in San Francisco in the 1860s and several of them have survived. Most famous is the McElroy Octagon House at 2645 Gough Street, built by William C. McElroy in 1861.

98

The Palace Hotel on the corner of Market and Montgomery was destroyed by fire following the Great Earthquake of 1906 and was completely rebuilt, opening to much acclaim on December 16, 1909

The San Francisco Graft Trials

Early 20th century San Francisco was a cesspool of corruption, and licenses and approvals of all sorts were for sale. US District Attorney Francis Heney vigorously an the investigation which resulted in the famous Graft Trials in 1906 to 1908. At the heart of the scandal were San Francisco Mayor Eugene Schmitz and his attorney Abe Ruef, who organised the scam, acting on Schmitz's behalf. Schmitz approved all contracts and received huge sums from business owners which he distributed to members of the city's Board of Supervisors. Ruef was found guilty and served four years in San Quentin prison, where he wrote a series of articles exposing the scheme, and the names of bribers and bribees. Mayor Schmitz was also found guilty, but did not serve any time in jail. All the business owners and members of the Board of Supervisors implicated in the case received immunity in return for testimony against Ruef and Schmitz. The San Francisco Call, in an editorial published on October 22, 1906, expressed the general sentiment of San Francisco towards the investigation. The article introduces the wonderful word "boodling":

"San Francisco will welcome the undertaking by Mr. Francis J. Heney of the duty to search out and bring to justice the official boodlers and their brokers that afflict the body politic. Public opinion is unanimous in the belief that Supervisors have been bribed and that administrative functions such as those of the Board of Works and the Health Board have been peddled in secret market. Even the Board of Education is not exempted from suspicion.

"These convictions, prevailing in the public mind, call for verification or refutation. The sudden affluence of certain members of the Board of Supervisors, the current and generally credited reports that the United Railroads paid upward of $500,000 in bribes to grease the way of its overhead trolley franchise, the appearance of public officials in the guise of capitalists making large investments in skating rinks and other considerable enterprises — these and other lines of investigation demand the probe. If there has been no dishonesty in office the officials should be the first to insist on a thorough inquiry.

"If it is true, as we believe, that official boodling has been the practice, a systematic inquiry will surely uncover the crimes. It is impossible to commit such offenses where so many are concerned without leaving some trace that can be followed and run to earth. The crimes of the gaspipe thugs seemed for the moment hidden in impenetrable mystery, but patient search discovers the trail that leads to conviction. Criminals are rarely men of high intelligence. They betray themselves at one or other turn of their windings. We are convinced that some of our Supervisors and not a few of the executive officials appointed by Schmitz are in no degree superior in point of intelligence and moral sense to the gaspipe robbers.

"Mr. Heney's record as a remorseless and indefatigable prosecutor of official rascals is known. He will have the assistance in his new work of Mr. William J. Burns, who did so much to bring to light the Oregon land frauds. Those crimes were surrounded and protected by fortifications of political influence that were deemed impregnable. When the inquiry was first undertaken nobody believed it would ever come to anything. It was a slow business, even as the mills of the gods grind slowly, but if fine the grist of the criminal courts of Oregon is large and satisfying.

"The people of San Francisco have been sorely tried. Fire and earthquake we cannot help, but the unhappy city has been made the prey of a set of conscienceless thieves who have done nothing since our great calamity beyond promoting schemes to fill their own pockets. Our streets, our sewers, our schools and our public buildings have been neglected, but the sale of permits and franchises, the working of real estate jobs and the market for privileges of every variety have been brisk and incessant. Officials have grown rich: Some of them are spending money like a drunken sailor. It is time for housecleaning and a day of reckoning. Heney and Burns will put the question: 'Where did they get it?'"

Serious Business

The opening to the novel Blindfolded, *written by Earle Ashley Walcott and published in 1907.*

A city of hills with a fringe of houses crowning the lower heights; half-mountains rising bare in the background and becoming real mountains as they stretched away in the distance to right and left; a confused mass of buildings coming to the water's edge on the flat; a forest of masts, ships swinging in the stream, and the streaked, yellow, gray-green water of the bay taking a cold light from the setting sun as it struggled through the wisps of fog that fluttered above the serrated sky-line of the city — these were my first impressions of San Francisco.

The wind blew fresh and chill from the west with the damp and salt of the Pacific heavy upon it, as I breasted it from the forward deck of the ferry steamer, El Capitan. As I drank in the air and was silent with admiration of the beautiful panorama that was spread before me, my companion touched me on the arm.

"Come into the cabin," he said. "You'll be one of those fellows who can't come to San Francisco without catching his death of cold, and then lays it on to the climate instead of his own lack of common sense. Come, I can't spare you, now I've got you here at last. I wouldn't lose you for a million dollars."

"I'll come for half the money," I returned, as he took me by the arm and led me into the close cabin.

My companion, I should explain, was Henry Wilton, the son of my father's cousin, who had the advantages of a few years of residence in California, and sported all the airs of a pioneer. We had been close friends through boyhood and youth, and it was on his offer of employment that I had come to the city by the Golden Gate.

"What a resemblance!" I heard a woman exclaim, as we entered the cabin. "They must be twins."

"There, Henry," I whispered, with a laugh; "you see we are discovered." Though our relationship was not close we had been cast in the mold of some common ancestor. We were so nearly alike in form and feature as to perplex all but our intimate acquaintances, and we had made the resemblance the occasion of many tricks in our boyhood days.

Henry had heard the exclamation as well as I. To my surprise, it appeared to bring him annoyance or apprehension rather than amusement.

"I had forgotten that it would make us conspicuous," he said, more to himself than to me, I thought; and he glanced through the cabin as though he looked for some peril.

"We were used to that long ago," I said, as we found a seat. "Is the business ready for me? You wrote that you thought it would be in hand by the time I got here."

"We can't talk about it here," he said in a low tone. "There is plenty of work to be done. It's not hard, but, as I wrote you, it needs a man of pluck and discretion. It's delicate business, you understand, and dangerous if you can't keep your head. But the danger won't be yours. I've got that end of it."

"Of course you're not trying to do anything against the law?" I said.

"Oh, it has nothing to do with the law," he replied with an odd smile. "In fact, it's a little matter in which we are—well, you might say—outside the law."

I gave a gasp at this disturbing suggestion, and Henry chuckled as he saw the consternation written on my face. Then he rose and said:

"Come, the boat is getting in."

"But I want to know—" I began.

"Oh, bother your 'want-to-knows.' It's not against the law—just outside it, you understand. I'll tell you more of it when we get to my room. Give me

A catamaran at the San Francisco Yacht Club, 1877

103

that valise. Come along now." And as the boat entered the slip we found ourselves at the front of the pressing crowd that is always surging in and out of San Francisco by the gateway of the Market-Street ferry.

As we pushed our way through the clamoring hack-drivers and hotel-runners who blocked the entrance to the city, I was roused by a sudden thrill of the instinct of danger that warns one when he meets the eye of a snake. It was gone in an instant, but I had time to trace effect to cause. The warning came this time from the eyes of a man, a lithe, keen-faced man who flashed a look of triumphant malice on us as he disappeared in the waiting-room of the ferry-shed. But the keen face, and the basilisk glance were burned into my mind in that moment as deeply as though I had known then what evil was behind them.

My companion swore softly to himself.

"What's the matter?" I asked.

"Don't look around," he said. "We are watched."

"The snake-eyed man?"

"Did you see him, too?" His manner was careless, but his tone was troubled. "I thought I had given him the slip," he continued. "Well, there's no help for it now."

"Are we to hunt for a hiding-place?" I asked doubtfully.

"Oh, no; not now. I was going to take you direct to my room. Now we are going to a hotel with all the publicity we can get. Here we are."

"Internaytional! Internaytional!" shouted a runner by our side. "Yes, sir; here you are, sir. Free 'bus, sir." And in another moment we were in the lumbering coach, and as soon as the last lingering passenger had come from the boat we were whirling over the rough pavement, through a confusing maze of streets, past long rows of dingy, ugly buildings, to the hotel.

Though the sun had but just set, the lights were glimmering in the windows along Kearny Street as we stepped from the 'bus, and the twilight was rapidly fading into darkness.

"A room for the night," ordered Henry, as we entered the hotel office and saluted the clerk.

"Your brother will sleep with you?" inquired the clerk.

"Yes."

"That's right—if you are sure you can tell which is which in the morning," said the clerk, with a smile at his poor joke.

Henry smiled in return, paid the bill, took the key, and we were shown to our room. After removing the travel-stains, I declared myself quite ready to dine.

"We won't need this again," said Henry, tossing the key on the bureau as we left. "Or no, on second thought," he continued, "it's just as well to leave the door locked. There might be some inquisitive callers." And we betook ourselves to a hasty meal that was not of a nature to raise my opinion of San Francisco.

"Are you through?" asked my companion, as I shook my head over a melancholy piece of pie, and laid down my fork. "Well, take your bag. This door — look pleasant and say nothing."

He led the way to the bar and then through a back room or two, until with a turn we were in a blind alley. With a few more steps we found ourselves in a back hall which led into another building. I became confused after a little, and lost all idea of the direction in which we were going. We mounted one flight of stairs, I remember, and after passing through two or three winding hallways and down another flight, came out on a side street.

After a pause to observe the street before we ventured forth, Henry said:

"I guess we're all right now. We must chance it, anyhow." So we dodged along in the shadow till we came to Montgomery Street, and after a brief walk, turned into a gloomy doorway and mounted a worn pair of stairs.

The house was three stories in height. It stood on the corner of an alley, and the lower floor was intended for a store or saloon; but a renting agent's sign and a collection of old show-bills ornamenting the dirty windows testified that it was vacant. The liquor business appeared to be overdone in that quarter, for across the alley, hardly twenty feet away, was a saloon; across Montgomery Street was another; and two more held out their friendly lights on the corner of the street above.

In the saloons the disreputability was cheerful, and cheerfully acknowledged with lights and noise, here of a broken piano, there of a wheezy accordion, and, beyond, of a half-drunken man singing or shouting a ribald song. Elsewhere it was sullen and dark, — the lights, where there were lights, glittering through chinks, or showing the outlines of drawn curtains.

"This isn't just the place I'd choose for entertaining friends," said Henry, with a visible relief from his uneasiness, as we climbed the worn and dirty stair.

"Oh, that's all right," I said, magnanimously accepting his apology.

"It doesn't have all the modern conveniences," admitted Henry as we stumbled up the second flight, "but it's suitable to the business we have in hand, and —"

"What's that?" I exclaimed, as a creaking, rasping sound came from the hall below.

We stopped and listened, peering into the obscurity beneath.

Nothing but silence. The house might have been a tomb for any sign of life that showed within it.

"It must have been outside," said Henry. "I thought for a moment perhaps—" Then he checked himself. "Well, you'll know later," he concluded, and opened the door of the last room on the right of the hall.

As we entered, he held the door ajar for a full minute, listening intently. The obscurity of the hall gave back nothing to eye or ear, and at last he closed the door softly and touched a match to the gas.

The room was at the rear corner of the building. There were two windows, one looking to the west, the other to the north and opening on the narrow alley.

"Not so bad after you get in," said Henry, half as an introduction, half as an apology.

"It's luxury after six days of railroading," I replied.

"Well, lie down there, and make the most of it, then," he said, "for there may be trouble ahead." And he listened again at the crack of the door.

"In Heaven's name, Henry, what's up?" I exclaimed with some temper. "You're as full of mysteries as a dime novel."

Henry smiled grimly.

"Maybe you don't recognize that this is serious business," he said.

An old San Francisco residence. Looking out at the Golden Gate with the Presidio in the distance

Worse Than Sodom and Gomorrah

Ambrose Bierce was an American journalist and writer noted for taking a blackly critical view on issues. His cynical lexicon, The Devil's Dictonary, was published in 1906 and remains in print. Here is comment on San Francisco from a letter written by Bierce dated June 25, 1907.

I'd never set foot in San Francisco. Of all the Sodoms and Gomorrahs in our modern world, it is the worst. There are not ten righteous (and courageous) men there. It needs another quake, another whiff of fire and more than all else a steady trade wind of grapeshot.

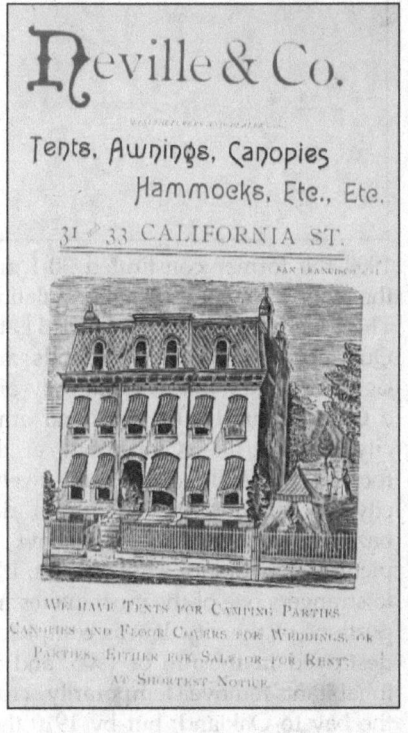

California, more than any other part of the Union, is a country
by itself, and San Francisco a capital.
James Bryce, The American Commonwealth, *1901.*

> "San Francisco has only one drawback—'tis hard to leave."
> *Rudyard Kipling*

Keeper of the Doors

The Encyclopædia Britannica Eleventh Edition, *published in 1911, is a massive 29-volume reference work that for reasons related to the shift from being a British to an American publication around that time, is in the public domain. The work is invaluable in providing a view on perceptions and prejudices of the world at the end of an era, just before World War I changed everything. Here is an excerpt from the Encyclopedia's entry on San Francisco.*

THE

ENCYCLOPÆDIA BRITANNICA

A

DICTIONARY

OF

ARTS, SCIENCES, LITERATURE AND GENERAL INFORMATION

ELEVENTH EDITION

VOLUME I
A to ANDROPHAGI

NEW YORK
THE ENCYCLOPÆDIA BRITANNICA COMPANY
1910

San Francisco, the chief seaport and the metropolis of California and the Pacific Coast, the tenth city in population (1910) of the United States, and the largest and most important city W. of the Missouri river, situated centrally on the coast of the state in 37 47′ 22-55′ N. and 122 25′ 40-76* W., at the end of a peninsula, with the ocean on one side and the Bay of San Francisco on the other. Pop. (1850), 34,000; (1890), 298,997; (1900), 342,782, of whom 116,885 were foreign-born and 17,404 coloured (mainly Asiatics); (1910) 416,912 ...

Population. The population of San Francisco increased in successive decades alter 1850 by 67-6, 16-3, 56-5, 27-8, i^-6and 21-6%. The population is very cosmopolitan. Germans and Irish are not so numerous here, relatively, as in various other cities, although in 1900 the former constituted 30-1 and the latter 13-6% of the total population. There is a large Ghetto, a so-called Latin Quarter, where Spanish sounds and signs are dominant, a Little Italy and a Chinese quarter of which no other city has the like. Chinatown, at the foot of Nob Hill, covers some twelve city blocks, and with its temples, rich bazaars, strange life and show of picturesque colours and customs, it is to strangers one of the most interesting portions of the city. It was completely destroyed in the fire of 1906, and its inhabitants removea temporarily across the bay to Oakland, but by 1910 the_ quarter had been practically rebuilt jn an improved manner, yet retaining its markedly oriental characteristics. The new Chinatown gained considerably in sanitation and in the housing of its commercial establishments. San Francisco has naturally been the centre of anti-Chinese agitation. The success of the exclusion laws is seen (though this is not the sole cause) in the decrease of the Chinese population from 24,613 to 13,954 between 1890 and 1900. The Japanese numbered 1781 in 1900 and have very rapidly increased. The question of their admission to the public schools, rivalry in labour and trade, and other racial antagonisms attendant on their rapid increase in numbers, created conflicts that at one time seriously involved the relations of the two countries. Two Chinese papers are published. More than half of the daily papers are foreign language ...

Earthquakes had been common but of little importance in California until 1906. In more than a century there had been three shocks called " destructive " (1839, 1865, 1868) and four " exceptionally severe " at San Francisco, besides very many light shocks or tremors. The worst was that of 1868; it caused five deaths, and cracked a dozen old buildings. Heavy earthquake shocks on the morning of the i8th of April 1906, followed by a fire which lasted three days, and a few slighter shocks, practically destroyed the business section of the city and some adjoining districts. The heaviest shock began at 12 minutes 6 seconds past 5 o'clock a.m., Pacific standard time, and lasted 1 minute 5 seconds. Minor shocks occurred at intervals for several days. The earthquake did serious damage throughout the coast region of California from Humboldt county to the southern end of Fresno county, a belt about 50 m. wide. The damage by earthquake to buildings in San Francisco was, however, small in comparison to that wrought by the fire which began soon after the principal shock on the morning of the 18th. About half the population of the city, it was estimated, spent the nights while the fire was in progress out of doors, with practically no shelter. Some 200,000 camped in Golden Gate Park and 50,000 in the presidio military reservation. The difficulty of checking the fire was increased through the breaking of the water-mains by the earthquake, draining the principal reservoirs. Traffic by street cars was made impossible by the twisting of the tracks. To stop the fire rows of buildings were dynamited. In this way many fine mansions on Van Ness Avenue were destroyed, and the westward advance of the conflagration was stopped at Franklin Street, one block west. General Frederick Funston, in command at the presidio, with the Federal troops under him, assumed control, and the city was put under military law, the soldiers assisting in the work of salvage and relief. On the 21st the fire was reported under control.

> "You know what it is? It's a golden handcuff with the key thrown away."
> *John Steinbeck*

The Yellow Fiends

Penny dreadful crime stories were popular as the 19th century shifted gears into the 20th century, and San Francisco and its inscrutible Oriental residents were a basis for many stories. One, called The Bradys After A Chinese Princess Or, The Yellow Fiends Of 'Frisco, *was written by Francis Worcester Doughty and published in a weekly magazine in 1911. Here is the opening, dripping with mystery in the darker regions of San Francisco's waterfront.*

One foggy night a few years since at something after two o'clock, a good-sized motor boat containing five men might have been seen cruising close in to the water-front line of lower San Francisco.

Three of the occupants were big, husky fellows, who sat idly in the boat looking like men waiting to be called upon to act and prepared for any emergency. A good-looking young fellow in his twenties was attending to engineer's duty, while astern sat an elderly man of striking appearance and peculiar dress. He wore a long, blue coat with brass buttons, an old-fashioned stock and stand-up collar, and a big white hat with an unusually broad brim. Clearly he was the leader of this outfit, whatever their business might be out there on the silent bay

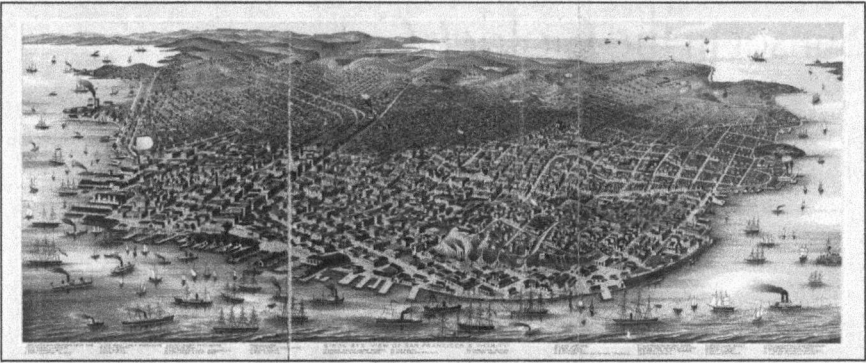

in the early morning hours.

He was a man accustomed to command, being none other than the world-famous detective, Old King Brady, chief of the Brady Detective Bureau of Union Square, New York. And having made this statement, we need scarcely add that the young man in charge of the boat was his partner, Young King Brady, second in skill as a detective only to his great chief.

The detective had been ordered to San Francisco on special duty by the United States Secret Service Bureau. Information had been received of the intention of certain Chinamen to run in opium on a large scale, dodging the duty due to Uncle Sam.

The information, while definite and reliable, was still vague. Details were lacking, yet it was known that there was surely going to be something doing in the line during this particular week, and that whatever was done would take place in the neighborhood of the India Basin.

This made the fourth night the Bradys had been on the watch with three local Secret Service men as their aides. It was discouraging work. Nothing had happened. The weak point of the undertaking was the lack of knowledge as to the particular ship or steamer on which the opium was expected to arrive. Two steamers had arrived from China this week, one regular liner and one tramp. Three sailing vessels had also come in, all from Chinese ports. Yet it was by no means certain that the opium would enter the harbor of San Francisco in that way. It is quite the custom with captains of English tramp steamers, and also with those of sailing vessels, to drop opium overboard in sealed rubber bags while off the Farraleone Islands. Such bags are picked up by fishing schooners on hand for the purpose, and by them landed as best they can. A close watch for such operations in this particular instance was being kept by a special revenue cutter outside the Golden Gate....

Sunset in the Golden Gate

This is a poem from the book Byways Around San Francisco Bay, *published in 1915 by W. E. Hutchinson and illustrated by the author. This is the Golden Gate pre-bridge, of course.*

When day is done there falls a solemn hush:
The birds are silent in their humble nest.
Then comes the Master Artist with his brush,
And paints with brilliant touch the golden west.

The blended colors sweep across the sky,
And add a halo at the close of day.
Their roseate hues far-reaching banners fly,
And gild the restless waters of the bay.

Mount Tamalpais stands in purple 'tire
Against the background, Phoenixlike, ornate:
Apollo drives his chariot of fire
Between the portals of the Golden Gate.

No other hand than His who rules on high,
Could wield the brush and spread such bright array
Upon the outstretched canvas of the sky,
Then draw the curtain of departing day.

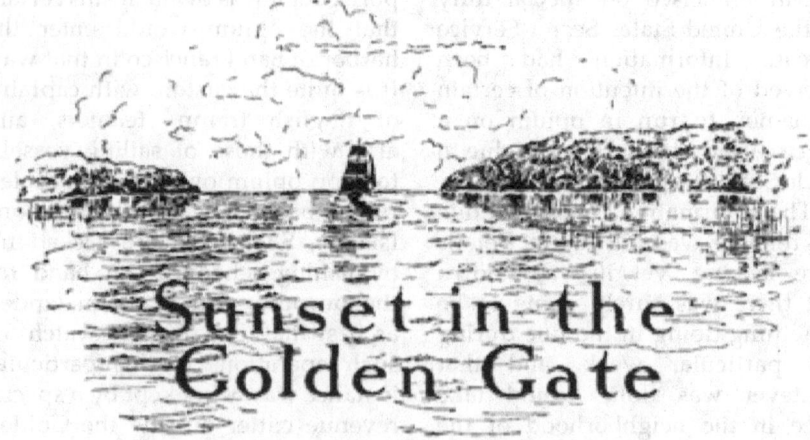

Scars and Trophies

The author and poet Louis John Stellman wrote a novel about San Francisco called Port
O' Gold, *published in 1922, which placed the city in an exalted position. He began the
book with a poetic paean:*

TO THE CITY OF MY ADOPTION AND REBIRTH
SAN FRANCISCO

Oft from my window have I seen the day
Break o'er thy roofs and towers like a dream
In mystic silver, mirrored by the Bay,
Bedecked with shadow craft ... and then a gleam
Of golden sunlight cleaving swiftly sure
Some narrow cloud-rift--limning hill or plain
With flecks of gypsy-radiance that endure
But for the moment and are gone again.

Then I have ventured on thy strident streets,
Mid whir of traffic in the vibrant hour
When Commerce with its clashing cymbal greets
The mighty Mammon in his pomp of power....
And in the quiet dusk of eventide,
As wearied toilers quit the marts of Trade,
Have I been of their pageant--or allied
With Passion's revel in the Night Parade.
Oh, I have known thee in a thousand moods
And lived a thousand lives within thy bounds;
Adventured with the throng that laughs or broods,
Trod all thy cloisters and thy pleasure grounds,
Seen thee, in travail from the fiery torch,
Betrayed by Greed, smirched by thy sons' disgrace--
Rise with a spirit that no flame can scorch

To make thyself a new and honored place.
Ah, Good Gray City! Let me sing thy song
Of western splendor, vigorous and bold;
In vice or virtue unashamed and strong--
Stormy of mien but with a heart of gold!
I love thee, San Francisco; I am proud
Of all thy scars and trophies, praise or blame
And from thy wind-swept hills I cry aloud
The everlasting glory of thy name.

Constant Deaths and Sky-High Wages

A description of the city from Martin Johnson's Through the South Seas with Jack London, *published in 1913.*

As for Frisco itself, it looked hopeless. Hundreds of tons of the wreckage had been cleared away, but hundreds of tons still remained. Some few buildings had already been erected. Most of them were stores, little wooden affairs, knocked together until better could be built. The fire and quake had ruined the pavements, and the streets were nothing but great pools of water and mud. A man was actually drowned in one of these pools while walking down Market Street. There were constant deaths by accidents; walls, frail and fissured, had a trick of collapsing and letting down their bushels of brick and stone on the heads of such as were in the streets; the street-car service was badly muddled, and several persons were killed while riding the precarious conveyances. . . . wages were sky-high; yet workmen still complained and struck for more. At the time I was there, the bricklayers, who were getting ten dollars a day, struck for twelve dollars and a half.

Twice

`The greatness of Rome is somehow associated - whether correctly or not - with the fact that it was built on seven hills. How much greater, then, should San Francisco be, standing on fourteen hills?' . . . The answer, so it seemed to me, surely must be `Twice.'

A.G. Macdonell, A Visit to America, *1935.*

Overview of the PanPac exhibition, 1915

War-Bred Pestilence

A pandemic swept the world in 1918 during the closing months of World War One, an influenza strain that killed more than 50 million people. The city of San Francisco came through the first wave in the spring almost untouched, although 3,500 people died in the second and third waves later that year. The writer John Barry, in his important book The Great Influenza, *published in 2005, takes up the story:*

In fact, of all the major cities in the country, San Francisco had confronted the fall wave most honestly and efficiently. That may have had something to do with its surviving, and rebuilding itself after the massive earthquake of only a dozen years before. Now on September 21 public health director William Hassler quarantined all naval installations, even before any cases surfaced in them or in the city. He mobilized the entire city in advance, recruiting hundreds of drivers and volunteers and dividing the city into districts, each with its own medical personnel, phones, transport and supply, and emergency hospitals in schools and churches. He closed public places. And far from the usual assurances that the disease was ordinary "la grippe," on October 22 the mayor, Hassler, the Red Cross, the Chamber of Commerce, and the Labor Council jointly declared in a full-page newspaper ad, "Wear a mask and save your life!" claiming that it was "99% proof against influenza." By October 26, the Red Cross had distributed one hundred thousand masks. Simultaneously, while local facilities geared up to produce vaccine, thousands of doses of a vaccine made by a Tufts scientist were raced across the continent on the country's fastest train. In San Francisco, people felt a sense of control. Instead of the paralyzing fear found in too many other communities, it seemed to inspire.

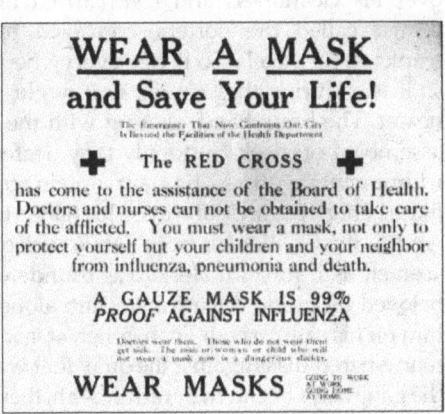

WEAR A MASK
and Save Your Life!

The Emergency That Now Confronts Our City
Is Beyond the Facilities of the Health Department

✚ The RED CROSS ✚

has come to the assistance of the Board of Health.
Doctors and nurses can not be obtained to take care
of the afflicted. You must wear a mask, not only to
protect yourself but your children and your neighbor
from influenza, pneumonia and death.

A GAUZE MASK IS 99%
PROOF AGAINST INFLUENZA

Doctors wear them. Those who do not wear them
get sick. The man or woman or child who will
not wear a mask now is a dangerous slacker.

WEAR MASKS

"San Francisco itself is art, above all literary art. Every block is a short story, every hill a novel. Every home a poem, every dweller within immortal. That is the whole truth."
Dramatist and writer William Saroyan, born in California in 1908 and died there in 1980.

The Gentleman From San Francisco

*This is the title of a story published in 1922
and written by the Russian novelist Ivan
Alekseyevich Bunin, who was the first
Russian to win the Nobel Prize for Literature.
It was translated by D.H. Lawrence and
S.S. Koteliansky, and tells of a man from
San Francisco who travels to Naples in Italy
and meets with a certain situation. Here is
an excerpt which has an interesting take on
the American personality filtered through a
Russian brain:*

Like all Americans, he was very liberal with
his money when traveling. And like all of
them, he believed in the full sincerity and
good-will of those who brought his food
and drinks, served him from morn till night,
anticipated his smallest desire, watched
over his cleanliness and rest, carried his
things, called the porters, conveyed his
trunks to the hotels. So it was everywhere,
so it was during the voyage, so it ought to be in Naples. Naples grew and drew
nearer. The brass band, shining with the brass of their instruments, had already
assembled on deck. Suddenly they deafened everybody with the strains of their
triumphant rag-time. The giant captain appeared in full uniform on the bridge, and
like a benign pagan idol waved his hands to the passengers in a gesture of welcome.
And to the Gentleman from San Francisco, as well as to every other passenger, it
seemed as if for him alone was thundered forth that rag-time march, so greatly
beloved by proud America; for him alone the Captain's hand waved, welcoming
him on his safe arrival. Then, when at last the Atlantis entered port and veered her
many-tiered mass against the quay that was crowded with expectant people, when
the gangways began their rattling--ah, then what a lot of porters and their assistants
in caps with golden galloons, what a lot of all sorts of commissionaires, whistling
boys, and sturdy ragamuffins with packs of postcards in their hands rushed to
meet the Gentleman from San Francisco with offers of their services! With what
amiable contempt he grinned at those ragamuffins as he walked to the automobile
of the very same hotel at which the prince would probably put up, and calmly
muttered between his teeth, now in English, now in Italian--"Go away! Via!"

> I have always been rather better treated in San Francisco than I actually deserved.
>
> *Mark Twain*

"WHEN THE GOLDEN GATE IS GOLDEN", SAN FRANCISCO, CALIF.

San Francisco is one of the great cultural plateaus of the world — one of the really urbane communities in the United States — one of the truly cosmopolitan places and for many, many years, it always has had a warm welcome for human beings from all over the world.

Duke Ellington

117

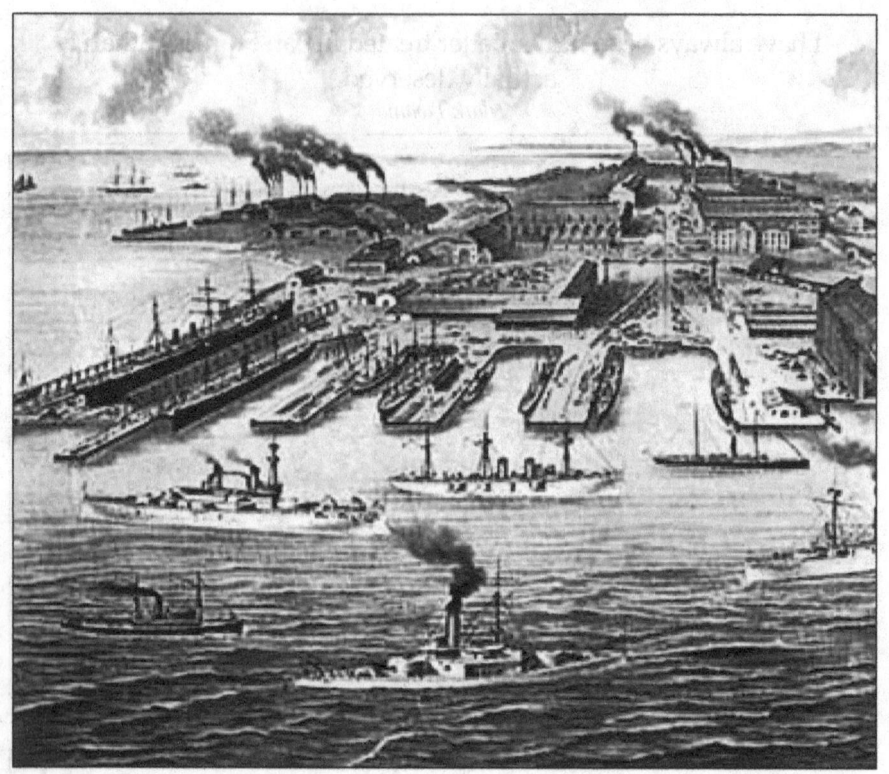

A view from the early 1900s of the Union Iron Works with some of the naval ships it produced

The Port and the Piers

The Port of San Francisco was the busiest port on the west coast of the United States until the 1920s, when Los Angeles eclipsed it. The piers that extend out into the bay, up to Pier 70, are a monument to the vast quantities of freight that passed through this port, particularly in the late 19th century. The most famous of the piers today is Pier 39, a must-see tourist attraction, but it was only in the late 1970s that it was redeveloped and opened. It was not until 1990 that the sea lions decided to make their home in the vicinity. Also famous is Fisherman's Wharf, around the area of Pier 35, which takes its name from the Italian fishermen who settled there and operated fishing boats following the Gold Rush.

Coit Tower

Coit Tower on top of Telegraph Hill is 210 feet (64 m) in height and was built in 1933 using funds donated to the city by wealthy socialite Lillian Coit, who died in 1929. The tower is a classic art deco design and was built using reinforced concrete, featuring 29 fresco murals. The symbolic significance of the tower is presumably the same as for all other towers constructed by human beings.

COIT MEMORIAL, TELEGRAPH HILL, SAN FRANCISCO, CALIF.   29

© STANLEY A. PILTZ

The 1934 Strikes

A series of strikes hit the ports along the west coast of the United States in 1934, with sailors and longshoremen striking to achieve unionization. The wave of protests included a four-day general strike in San Francisco. Although they were put down, the protests did eventually lead to unionization of workers at the ports.

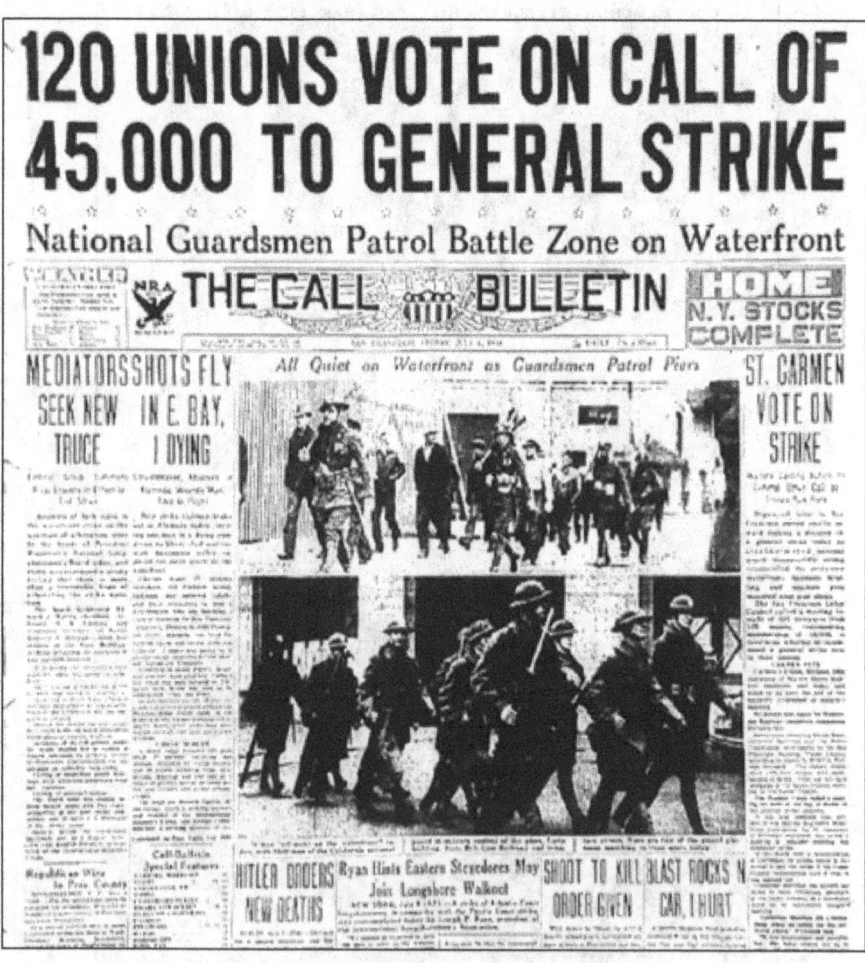

July 15, 1934: San Francisco News Call Bulletin

San Francisco, 1934. Armistice Day parade on Market Street

China and the 9th Circuit Court

The United States Court of Appeals for the Ninth Circuit is the largest of the appeals jurisdictions in the United States and is based in San Francisco, hearing appeals on cases from Alaska to Arizona, and also from Guam and the Northern Marianas.

From 1906 to 1943, it was also the appellate court for cases heard in the US Court for China which had exclusive jurisdiction over US citizens in China during that era. The US Court for China was based in Shanghai but travelled on circuit around China. There were no jury trials, the judge was the sole arbiter of law and fact. Congress had provided that "United States Law" applied in China. Most law in America is state or local territorial law. In order to avoid gaps in the law, the Ninth Circuit developed a theory that the law of two federal territories, Alaska and Washington DC, was "United States Law" and therefore applied in China.

Memorable cases from China heard by the court included an appeal by the US District Attorney for China, Leonard Husar, against his conviction for corruption (Husar claimed he had made the money smuggling guns!); an appeal by US lawyer William Fleming who had campaigned against the over-centralisation of power in the hands of the judge. The judge, Charles Lobingier, sentenced Fleming to six months imprisonment for accusing Lobingier of conspiring against him; and a case involving insurance claims in Hankow where the court had to decide whether, following their successful Northern Expedition in 1927 and 1928, the Nationalist Party was the legitimate government of China.

The very last appeal case was heard after the Pacific War started, and the Japanese occupied the Shanghai International Settlement and interned the judge and court staff. US Marine Gerald Casement had been convicted in 1941 of brutally murdering his infant step-son. Casement applied for a writ of habeas corpus in 1943 on the basis that he had not had a jury trial. The Ninth Circuit, in the understated tones of judicial opinions, provided a very practical reason for not ordering a new trial: "By reason of recent and present historical events involving Shanghai, the witnesses necessary to another trial for this petitioner could undoubtedly never in the future be presented before any court."

> "If you're alive, you can't be bored in San Francisco. If you're not alive, San Francisco will bring you to life."
> William Saroyan, American author awarded the Pulitzer Price in 1940

Dance, Then, Wild Guests

Vachel Lindsay was an American poet born in 1879, is known as the inventor of what is called "singing poetry." He believed that poetry should be sung in the same way as it was in the days of ancient Greece. Much of his material used mid-western themes, and he was known for a time as the "Prairie Troubador." This poem, dating from 1923, sings the praises of the city of San Francisco.

> Not by the earthquake daunted
> Nor by new fears made tame,
> Painting her face and laughing
> Plays she a new-found game.
> Here on her half-cool cinders
> 'Frisco abides in mirth,
> Planning the wildest splendor
> Ever upon the earth... .
>
> God loves this rebel city,
>
> Loves foemen brisk and game,
> Tho', just to please the angels.
> He may send down his flame.
> God loves the golden leopard
> Tho' he may spoil her lair,
> God smites, yet loves, the lion.
> God makes the panther fair.
>
> Dance then wild guests of 'Frisco,
> Yellow, bronze, white and red!
> Dance by the golden gateway -
> Dance tho' he smite you dead!

"The Bay Area is so beautiful, I hesitate to preach about heaven while I'm here."
American revivalist preacher Billy Graham

123

The Golden Gate Bridge

The Golden Gate Bridge is a suspension bridge which spans the Golden Gate strait, linking San Francisco Bay and the Pacific Ocean. The bridge, 4,200 feet (1,300m) in length, links the city of San Francisco to the north with Marin County to the south. It was completed in 1937 and until 1964, it was the world's longest suspension bridge. It is a symbol of San Francisco, but also of California and of the United States.

I will sing in San Francisco if I have to sing in the streets, for I know that the streets of San Francisco are free.
Statement by Luisa Tetrazzini , Italian soprano, in 1910 after she was blocked from singing in New York due to a legal dispute.

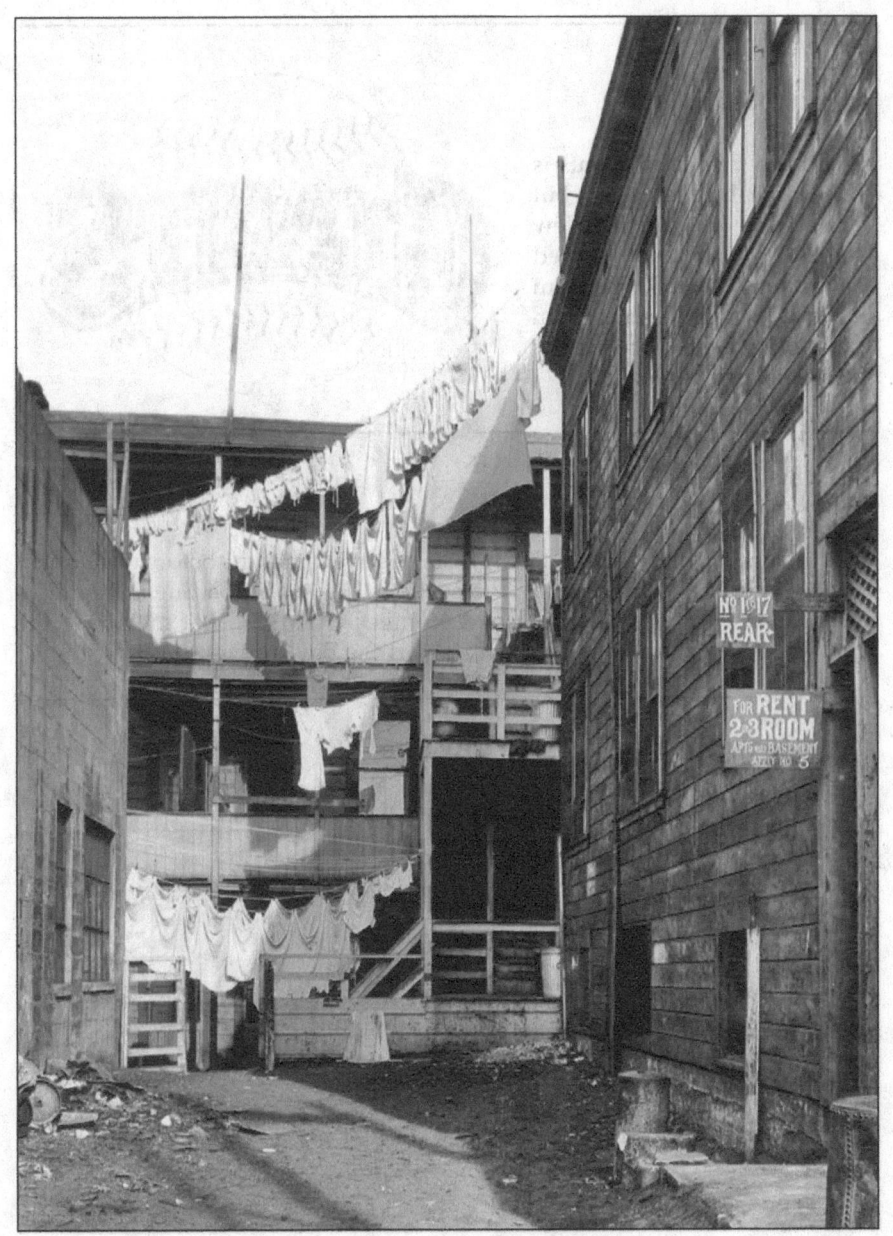

San Francisco, 1935

The Giants

The San Francisco Giants is the city's baseball team, but it started out as the New York Giants and moved west only in 1958. The team has won more games than any other team in the history of American baseball.

The Bay Bridge

The Oakland Bay Bridge opened in 1936, just a few months before the Golden Gate Bridge. It is composed of two sections linking Yerba Buena Island in the middle, with a total length of 4.46 miles (7.18 km), not including the approaches. It is known to locals simply as the Bay Bridge.

The Oakland bridge under construction

SFO

San Francisco airport was opened in 1927 on farm land leased from Ogden L. Mills and was called Mills Field Municipal Airport until 1931.

Old Gold Hill

Carl Crow was an American journalist from Missouri who moved to China in 1911 and lived there until he was forced out by the Japanese invasion of Shanghai in 1941. He wrote a couple of best-sellers explaining China to foreigners, and in this excerpt from his book 400 Million Customers, *he explains how Chinese handle foreign place names, including that of San Francisco.*

Not only the names of foreigners but the names of all foreign cities have to undergo these transformations and be christened anew in Chinese. In most cases the Chinese name is only an approximation of the sound of the 'foreign' name, but in other cases it is descriptive. London is known simply as 'British Capital'. San Francisco is 'Old Gold Hill', Honolulu is 'Sandalwood Island'. San Francisco was the focal point for early Chinese immigration, and the name was given it by the Chinese gold hunters. At about the same period the Hawaiian Islands provided China's supply of sandalwood. In Chinese songs San Francisco is known by the poetical name of 'Market of the Three Barbarian Tribes', referring to the Americans, British and Spanish who made up the greater part of the population of California in the Gold Rush days.

No Taxi

An excerpt from the Raymond Chandler novel, The Long Good-bye, *which was published in 1953. It was the sixth of Chandler's novels to feature the hard-bitten private investigator Philip Marlowe.*

' ... I been down and out myself. In Frisco. Nobody picked me up in no taxi either. There's one stony-hearted town.'

'San Francisco,' I said mechanically.

'I call it Frisco,' he said. 'The hell with them minority groups... '

... But Europe's Better

Cyril Connolly was an English writer born in 1903 (died 1974) who was famous and highly respected on both sides of the Atlantic, but never achieved commercial success. Here is his insightful but qualified take on San Francisco from his book American Injection, *published in 1947.*

San Francisco is a city of charming people and hideous buildings, mostly erected after the earthquake in the style of 1910, with a large Chinatown in which everything is fake - except the Chinese - with a tricky humid climate (though sunny in winter), and a maddening indecision in the vegetation - which can never decide if it belongs to the North or the South and achieves a Bournemouth compromise. Yet San Francisco and its surroundings probably represent the most attractive all-the-year-round alternative to Europe which the world can provide.

Shipyard ironworkers on break, 1943

The Rock

Alcatraz is an island in San Francisco Bay that served as the location of a federal prison from 1933 to 1963. Alcatraz had the reputation of being the toughest prison in the US penal system. It had previously been a military prison since 1868. It currently features the oldest lighthouse operating on the west coast of the United States. The prison is now closed and serves only as a tourist destination.

There were a total of 14 attempts at escapes by 36 prisoners, and not one of them is confirmed as having been successful. Most were captured or shot during the escapes, and five prisoners are listed as missing, presumed drowned.

A number of movies have been made about escapes from Alcatraz, including Birdman of Alcatraz (1962) starring Burt Lancaster, The Enforcer (1976), Escape from Alcatraz (1979), and The Rock (1996) starring Sean Connery.

Famous prisoners include Chicago crime boss Al Capone, Machine Gun Kelly and the "Birdman of Alcatraz", Robert Stroud. He was so named because of his interest in raised canaries. He spent 17 years in Alcatraz, having killed a barman in Alaska, and later stabbing a guard in Leavenworth prison in Kansas after he was refused a visit from his brother. He died in 1963 having never been granted permission to see the Burt Lancaster film about him.

Wish you were here!

"The Birdman of Alcatraz", Robert Stroud

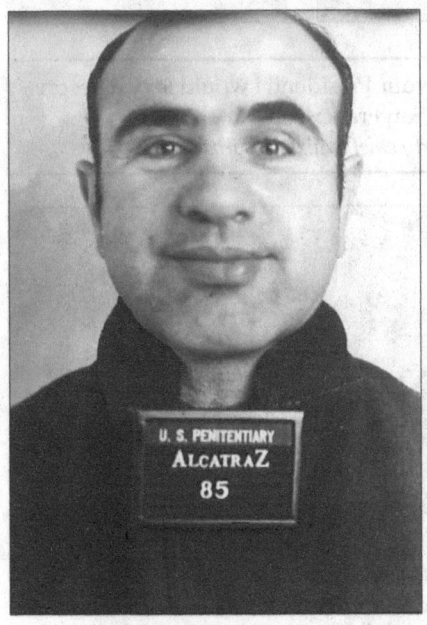

Al Capone

"Machine Gun" Kelly

> I always see about six scuffles a night when I come to San Francisco. That's one of the town's charms.
> *1940s film star, Errol Flynn*

> You are fortunate to live here. If I were your President, I would levy a tax on you for living in San Francisco.
> *Former Soviet Communist Party chief, Mikhail Gorbachev*

Seals Stadium, opened in 1931, was one of the iconic structures of early 20th century San Francisco, in the Mission District. It served as the home of the baseball teams the Shan Francisco Seals and later the San Francisco Giants before being demolished in 1959

An old San Francisco steakhouse

"What fetched me instantly (and thousands of other newcomers with me) was the subtle but unmistakable sense of escape from the United States."
H.L. Mencken, writer

A theater in the 1950s showing Chinese movies

Making-up in Chinatown

A shop assistant at the Tai Ping Company boutique on Grant Avenue demonstrates a giant Chinese fan to an interested customer

Vertical Drops

Humorist Dave Barry published a book in 1991 called The Only Travel Guide You'll Ever Need, *and San Francisco had to get a mention.*

... of course no trip to Northern California would be complete without a visit to San Francisco, whose romantic charm inspired the immortal Tony Bennett song, "Don't Mess with My Toot Toot." Be sure to join several tons of carbohydrate-bloated tourists for a ride on a quaint cable car, lurching up quaint "hills" that are actually 800-foot vertical drops as the cable-car driver dings the quaint little bell, sending out the cheerful message "ding-ading-ding," which is code for: "Look out, my cable is badly frayed."

Mutiny on the Caine

Herman Wouk won an Pulitzer Prize for his novel The Caine Mutiny, *published in 1951, which told the story of a mutiny on board a US destroyer in the Pacific during a typhoon in World War 2, as well as the trial that followed. The film of the book released in 1954 starring Humphrey Bogart was also a hit. What is the San Francisco connection? This passage is from the book.*

When Ensign Keith followed the bellboy into his room in the Mark Hopkins Hotel in San Francisco, he was struck at once by the view of the city in the sunset. The hills were twinkling. under a sky massed with clouds, pink in the west, fading to rose and violet in the east. The evening star shone clear, hanging low over the Golden Gate Bridge. Eastward the lamps were burning along the gray arches of the Oakland Bridge, a string of amber gems. The bellboy turned on lights, opened closets, and left Willie alone with the sunset and his bags. The new ensign stood by the window for a moment, stroking his gold stripe, and wondering at so much beauty and splendor so far from New York.

"Might as well unpack," he said to the evening star, and opened his pigskin valise. Most of his belongings were in a wooden crate in the hotel's check room. In the valise he carried only a few changes of clothes. On top of a layer of white shirts lay two mementos of his last hours in New York-a phonograph record and a letter.

> Somehow the great cities of America have taken their places in a mythology that shapes their destiny. Money lives in New York. Power sits in Washington. Freedom sips Cappuccino in a sidewalk cafe in San Francisco.
>
> *Joe Flower*

Twenty-three Skidoo

Philip K. Dick's outrageously wild science fiction stories included San Francisco quite often. He lived in the city from his youth and through much of his life, and went to school and briefly college in Berkeley. His novels include Blade Runner *and* Do Androids Dream of Electric Sheep? *This excerpt is from a novel called* Waterspider, *and features time travelers going back to San Francisco in the 1950s:*

With Gilly, the other member selected, Tozzo entered the time-dredge and seated himself at the controls. The Department of Archaeology had provided a full instruction manual, which lay open before him. As soon as Gilly had locked the hatch, Tozzo took the bull by the horns (a twentieth century expression) and started up the dredge.

Dials registered. They were spinning backward into time, back to 1954 and the San Francisco Pre-Cog Congress.

Beside him, Gilly practiced mid twentieth century phrases from a reference volume. "Diz muz be da blace. . ." Gilly cleared his throat. "Kilroy was here," he murmured. "Wha' hoppen? Like man, let's cut out; this ball's a drag." He shook his head. "I can't grasp the exact sense of these phrases," he apologized to Tozzo. "Twenty-three skidoo."

Now a red light glowed; the dredge was about to conclude its journey. A moment later its turbines halted.

They had come to rest on the sidewalk outside the Sir Francis Drake Hotel in downtown San Francisco.

On all sides, people in quaint archaic costumes dragged along on foot. And, Tozzo saw, there were no monorails; all the visible traffic was surface-bound. What a congestion, he thought, as he watched the automobiles and buses moving inch by inch along the packed streets. An official in blue waved traffic ahead as best he could, but the entire enterprise, Tozzo could see, was an abysmal failure.

"Time for phase two," Gilly said. But he, too, was gaping at the stalled surface vehicles. "Good grief," he said, "look at the incredibly short skirts of the women; why, the knees are virtually exposed. Why don't the women die of whisk virus?"

"I don't know," Tozzo said, "but I do know we've got to get into the Sir Francis Drake Hotel."

The Beat Generation

This movement, which lasted roughly from the 1940s to the 1960s, is intimately connected with San Francisco. It is associated most closely with Jack Kerouac and his book *On The Road*, published in 1957, in which the hero travels all the way across the United States aiming at San Francisco. The philosophy of the Beat Generation centred on rejection of standard social conventions in terms of career, family and lifestyle, and a "liberated" approach to artistic creation. The beatniks often explored Eastern religions. Key members of the group were poet Allen Ginsberg and William S. Burroughs, whose novel *Naked Lunch* was published in 1959. Other members of the community included Herbert Huncke and Lucien Carr. While New York was originally home for many of them, they gravitated to San Francisco, and merged in the mid-1960s into the hippies and the Youth Generation that had a much wider and deeper impact on global culture.

City Lights bookstore, a shrine to the Beat Generation

Rats in the Pantry

An excerpt from Jack Kerouac's On The Road, *published in 1957:*

There was an old rusty freighter out in the bay that was used as a buoy. Remi was all for rowing out to it, so one afternoon Lee Ann packed a lunch and we hired a boat and went out there. Remi brought some tools. Lee Ann took all her clothes off and lay down to sun herself on the flying bridge. I watched her from the poop. Remi went clear down to the boiler rooms below, where rats scurried around, and began hammering and banging away for copper lining that wasn't there. I sat in the dilapidated officer's mess. It was an old, old ship and had been beautifully appointed, with scrollwork in the wood, and built-n seachests. This was the ghost of the San Francisco of Jack London. I dreamed at the sunny messboard. Rats ran in the pantry. Once upon a time there'd been a blue-eyed sea captain dining in here.

Dr. A. O. Haslehurst

DENTIST

Office Hours,
9 to 12 and 1 to 5

337 Geary St., cor. Mason

Incomparable Blind Streets

The Beat Movement was centered on San Francisco and one of the leading lights of the push was the poet Allen Ginsberg, who shocked America with his manic, moving and magnificently obscene poem, "Howl," written in the city in 1955 and 1956. It is an indictment of the American capitalist system, but also a semi-autobiographical description of the Beat Movement and its members. Ginsberg's style is similar to that of Jack Kerouac - he mashes images into each other in a fast blur to build an impression for the listener or reader. The poem was published by City Lights bookstore in San Francisco, whose owner was jailed on obscenity charges as a result. Ginsberg performed it, often drunkenly, with great intensity. Here are the opening lines that presumably refer to San Francisco.

I saw the best minds of my generation destroyed by madness,
starving hysterical naked,
dragging themselves through the negro streets at dawn looking
for an angry fix,
angelheaded hipsters burning for the ancient heavenly connection
to the starry dynamo in the machinery of night,
who poverty and tatters and hollow-eyed and high sat up
smoking in the supernatural darkness of cold-water flats floating
across the tops of cities contemplating jazz,
who bared their brains to Heaven under the El and saw
Mohammedan angels staggering on tenement roofs illuminated,
who passed through universities with radiant cool eyes
hallucinating Arkansas and Blake-light tragedy among the
scholars of war,
who were expelled from the academies for crazy & publishing
obscene odes on the windows of the skull,
who cowered in unshaven rooms in underwear, burning their
money in wastebaskets and listening to the Terror through the wall,
who got busted in their pubic beards returning through Laredo
with a belt of marijuana for New York,
who ate fire in paint hotels or drank turpentine in Paradise Alley,
death, or purgatoried their torsos night after night
with dreams, with drugs, with waking nightmares, alcohol and
cock and endless balls,
incomparable blind streets of shuddering cloud and lightning in
the mind leaping toward poles of Canada & Paterson, illuminating
all the motionless world of Time between ...

Melting Pot

San Francisco has always been a place where many different cultures intersect, and the richness of its history and culture derive from that fact. Here is a table showing the percentages of the different races and nationalities in San Francisco's population based on information from **sfgeneology.com.**

Year	White (%)	Chinese (%)	Black (%)	Japanese (%)
1847 [3c]	375 (81.7)	–	10 (2.2)	–
1852 [3b]	35,531 (98.3)	–	323 (0.9)	–
1860 [6]	78,293 (94.0)	3,130 (3.8)	1,800 (2.2)	–
1870 [6]	136,059 (91.0)	11,728 (7.8)	1,330 (0.8)	302 (0.2)
1880	210,496 (90.0)	21,213 (9.1)	1,628 (0.7)	65 (0.0)
1890	270,696 (90.5)	25,833 (8.6)	1,847 (0.6)	590 (0.2)
1900	325,378 (94.9)	13,954 (4.1)	1,654 (0.4)	1,781 (0.5)
1910	400,014 (95.9)	10,582 (2.5)	1,642 (0.4)	4,518 (1.1)
1920	490,022 (96.7)	7,744 (1.5)	2,414 (0.4)	5,358 (1.0)
1930	620,891 (95.0)	16,303 (2.6)	3,803 (0.6)	6,250 (1.0)
1940	602,701 (95.0)	17,782 (2.8)	4,846 (0.8)	5,280 (0.8)
1950	693,888 (89.5)	24,813 (3.2)	43,502 (5.6)	5,579 (0.7)
1960	604,403 (81.6)	36,445 (4.9)	74,383 (10.0)	9,464 (1.3)
1970	409,285 (57.2)	58,696 (8.2)	96,078 (13.4)	11,705 (1.6)
1980	402,131 (59.2)	82,244 (12.1)	86,190 (12.7)	12,461 (1.8)

Heaven vs SFO

Herb Caen was a columnist on the San Francisco Chronicle *for nearly 60 years before his death in 1997, and won a Pulitzer Prize for his work, documenting the life of the city in a way that earned him the title the "voice and conscience" of San Francisco. He is credited with coining the word beatnik in the 1950s, and also with popularizing the word hippie during the "Summer of Love" in the city in 1967. Here is his the summation of his views on the city:*

"One day if I go to heaven ... I'll look around and say, 'It ain't bad, but it ain't San Francisco.'"

Doggie Diner

This was a famous San Francisco hamburger chain founded in 1948 which had at its height more than 30 outlets. It closed in 1986 under the onslaught of the larger fast food operators, but the dachshund sign is still close to the hearts of older San Franciscans.

Leave Frisco or Go Crazy

An excerpt from Jack Kerouac's On The Road, *published in 1957:*

Meanwhile I began going to Frisco more often; I tried everything in the books to make a girl. I even spent a whole night with a girl on a park bench, till dawn, without success. She was a blonde from Minnesota. There were plenty of queers. Several times I went to San Fran with my gun and when a queer approached me in a bar John I took out the gun and said, "Eh? Eh? What's that you say?" He bolted. I've never understood why I did that; I knew queers all over the country. It was just the loneliness of San Francisco and the fact that I had a gun. I had to show it to someone. I walked by a jewelry store and had the sudden impulse to shoot up the window, take out the finest rings and bracelets, and run to give them to Lee Ann. Then we could flee to Nevada together. The time was coming for me to leave Frisco or I'd go crazy.

The Friendliest City

Joe DiMaggio, one of the greatest baseball players of all time, is associated most closely with the city of New York. He played a total of 13 seasons for the New York Yankees. But he was also a great fan of San Francisco and had this to say about the city:

"I'm proud to have been a Yankee. But I have found more happiness and contentment since I came back home to San Francisco than any man has a right to deserve. This is the friendliest city in the world."

SF Bay Blues

One of the most recorded folk songs in the American repertoire, San Francisco Bay Blues was first-recorded by Jesse Fuller in 1952. The best-known versions include recordings by Eric Clapton, Bob Dylan and the Weavers. The Jesse Fuller version featuring a kazoo solo is particularly striking. The lyrics have proved to be flexible over the years, but here is part of one version:

I got the blues when my baby left me
By the San Francisco Bay,
Ocean liner, gone so far away.
Didn't mean to treat her so bad,
Best girl I ever has had.
Made me cry, like to make me die,
Wanna lay down and die.
Ain't got a nickel, ain't got a lousy dime,
If she don't come back, Lord, I think I'm gonna lose my mind.
If she ever comes back and stay,
Be another brand new day,
Walkin' with my baby down by San Francisco Bay.

Market Street, 1958

Cellars and Ballrooms

San Francisco's role in the development of rock and pop music was central to the genre's development. The following is a wonderfully succinct extract from Yeah Yeah Yeah, *a history of pop music written by Bob Stanley and published in 2014, which points to the comparisons with Liverpool, home of the Beatles.*

In many ways the San Francisco scene resembled the Liverpool beat boom of four years earlier. Both cities looked west, out to sea, separate from the rest of the country; both were known to be left-leaning and politically active; and both had a large dollop of civic pride which rubbed off on the young, who were happy to follow and support their local acts. Where Liverpool had cellars, San Francisco had ballrooms – the Avalon, the Carousel, the Longshoremen's Hall. Why San Francisco? It was a big city but small enough to sustain a scene – not manic like New York, not spread out like Los Angeles. One major difference from the Mersey boom, though, was that the Frisco bands were frequently not natives: Janis Joplin had arrived from Texas, Steve Miller from Canada. San Francisco was a postwar beacon. Drawn to the city as Dada's creators had been drawn to Zurich, incomers saw the city as neutral ground where you could walk the streets and not get your head kicked in for having hair that grazed your collar. The beat scene, which was centered around Lawrence Ferlinghetti's City Lights bookstore and publishing imprint, drew in small-town outcasts, intellectuals and would-be intellectuals, and they soon built a small hipster community in the low-rent Haight-Ashbury district.

A ticket from the last live concert ever performed by the Beatles, which took place in San Francisco's Candlestick Park on August 29, 1966. Their appearance on a roof in London in 1969 simply doesn't count

Far Out

Psychedelic rock concert posters were an art form that was developed in San Francisco in the mid-60s and spread around the world. The inspiration for the style were psychedelic experiences from such drugs as LSD and the style was used not only in rock concert posters, but also comic books, record album covers, advertisements, and the "underground" newspapers that were a part of the "scene" in those years. The style became emblematic of the era, now consigned as relics of an age delcared as "retro." Leading names amongst the San Francisco artists who developed the style proponents of the 1960s psychedelic art movement included San Francisco poster artists: Rick Griffin, Victor Moscoso, Bonnie MacLean, Stanley Mouse & Alton Kelley, and Wes Wilson.

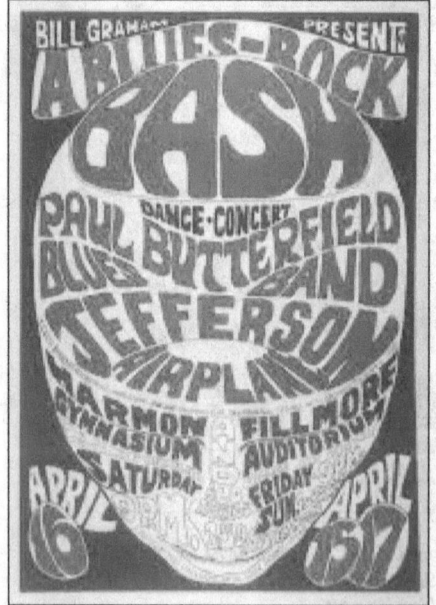

This vintage postcard shows the US Army Transport vessel Sherman docked at San Francisco's Pier No. 12

> When you emerge from the tunnel you are confronted with an unobstructed view of San Francisco.... and my first reaction was one of dismay. I did not want San Francisco to look like that, a cross between Manhattan and Chicago.
>
> *Ethel Mannin,* An American journey, *1967.*

Wooden Kimono

Tom Waits is a singer, songwriter and poet whose work often has a sense of Beat Generation San Francisco about it. The city doesn't overtly appear in his lyrics very often, but there is one reference in the wonderful song The One That Got Away, *from his 1976 album, Small Change:*

> ...And a wooden kimono
> That was all ready to drop
> In San Francisco Bay
> But he's mumbling something all about
> The one that got away

Songs about SF

San Francisco has been an attractive muse and topic for creative people work-
ing in all genres for over a century and a half. The role that San Francisco
played in the late 1960s as the launching pad for an entire youth music move-
ment made it a natural in terms of song references. Songs featuring San Fran-
cisco include:

- **I Left My Heart in San Francisco,** Tony Bennett's theme songs, written in 1953 and a hit for him in 1962
- **Lights** a tune from American rock band Journey, written by Steve Perry and Neal Schon and released in 1978
- **Let's Go to San Francisco**, a UK hit in 1967 for the pop group The Flower Pot Men, who were never heard of again
- **San Francisco Is a Lonely Town**, a minor hit in 1969 for its author Nashville songwriter Ben Peters
- **We Built This City** was an international hit in 1985 for Starship, a second re-incarnation of the seminal San Francisco band Jefferson Airplane. It was written by Elton John collaborator Bernie Taupin along with Martin Page, Dennis Lambert, and Peter Wolf
- **(Sittin' On) The Dock of the Bay** was co-written by Otis Redding and guitarist Steve Cropper. It was recorded by Redding in 1967 just before he died in a plane crash, and released in 1968 and was a global smash hit. Redding wrote the lyrics while sitting on a houseboat in Sausalito, California, and the Bay referred to can be no other than San Francisco's
- **San Franciscan Nights** was a hit in 1967 for Eric Burdon and The Animals, and was the biggest hit this new incarnation of the Animals was to have.
- **San Francisco (Be Sure to Wear Flowers in Your Hair)** was a hit in 1967 and 1968, riding the tide of the youth movement based in SF. It was written by John Phillips of The Mamas & the Papas, and sung by Scott McKenzie. It has been called the anthem of the 1960s counterculture movement
- **San Francisco (You Got Me)** was the first hit in 1978 for the Village People, a group which, while not based in the city, was closely associated with its gay scene
- **Taxi** is a song by Harry Chapin from 1972 that begins "It was raining hard in Frisco, I needed one more fare to make my night". It is the touching story of a chance encounter with an old love. Chapin, however, was born and died in New York City.

Zodiac Killer

This was the name of serial killer who terrorized San Francisco and other parts of the northern California starting in 1968. He was never caught. Exactly how many people he killed is not known, but at least seven are confirmed. The killer chose the name "Zodiac" himself, including it in various letters he wrote to local newspapers.

In August, 1969, the killer sent four letters to different newspapers, including the *San Francisco Chronicle* and the *San Francisco Examiner*, each containing a cryptogram message. Only part of one of the messages has ever been deciphered. A part of the deciphered message reads:

THE BEST PART OF IT IS THAE WHEN I DIE I WILL BE REBORN IN PARADICE AND THEI HAVE KILLED WILL BECOME MY SLAVES I WILL NOT GIVE YOU MY NAME BECAUSE YOU WILL TRY TO SLOI DOWN OR ATOP MY COLLECTIOG OF SLAVES FOR MY AFTERLIFE

(The spelling errors are as the message was deciphered).

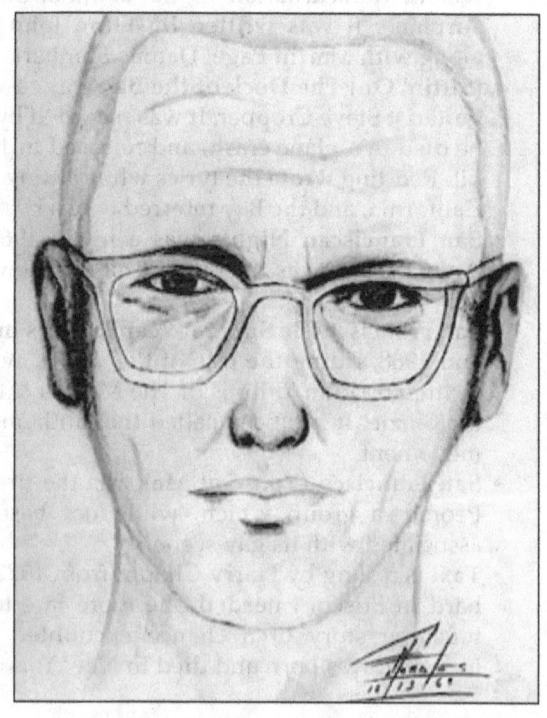

Zodiac went quiet for a number of years, then the *San Francisco Chronicle* received a letter from the Zodiac, postmarked January 29, 1974, praising Roman Polanski's film *The Exorcist* as "the best saterical comidy [sic] that I have ever seen". The letter ended the letter with a score: "Me = 37, SFPD = 0."

A number of suspects were investigated but no conclusive evidence was ever found. The case is considered "inactive" by the San Francisco Police Department (SFPD), although it remains an open case in some other jurisdictions including the city of Vallejo and in Napa County.

Bullitt

A must-see movie on San Francisco, *Bullitt* features one of the best car chases ever filmed, and stars one of the coolest of film stars, Steve McQueen. The film was shot entirely on location in San Francisco. The film's famous chase scene features Bullitt's 1968 Ford Mustang GT fastback and a 1968 Dodge Charger R/T. The chase scene lasts 10 minutes and 53 seconds, beginning close to Fisherman's Wharf at Columbus and Chestnut, then racing through midtown on Hyde and Laguna Streets, and ending outside the city at the Guadalupe Canyon Parkway in Brisbane.

43.–SAN FRANCISCO-OAKLAND BAY BRIDGE AND SAN FRANCISCO, CALIFORNIA

Exit The Dragon

Kung Fu star Bruce Lee was born in San Francisco at the Jackson Street Hospital in Chinatown on November 27, 1940 and he and his family left for Hong Kong in 1941. He returned to the US at the age of 18, having developed a physique and a kung fu martial arts style that was unique. He quickly became a superstar and his five movies were worldwide hits in the 1970s and the 1980s. Bruce's connection to San Francisco is symbolic of the role that the city has played in assimilating Asian and particularly Chinese influences into American life and consciousness. He died in Hong Kong on July 20, 1973, in circumstances that seem to relate to a combination of prescription and recreational drugs.

A key part of the Bruce Lee legend is a martial arts contest that took place in 1964 between him and another martial arts master in the greater San Francisco area, Wong Jack Man. At the time, Bruce was teaching martial arts in a studio in Chinatown and taking any students including non-Chinese. This incensed a certain member of the Chinese community who believed the fighting skills should be kept as their secret and not shared with Caucasians or others. They ordered him to stop and he refused. Wong Jack Man then issued an ultimatum, backed by basically all the martial arts masters of San Francisco Chinatown challenging Bruce to a one-on-one contest with the agreement being that if he lost, Bruce would have to give up teaching non-Chinese students. The fight took place in a Chinatown theater. It was no-holds-barred, and it lasted, according to Bruce's widow, only three minutes before his opponent was thrown to the ground and surrendered.

"Do you give up?" Bruce shouted.

"I give up," his opponent replied.

342 Minute Leaves

An excerpt from Tom Wolfe's `The Put-Together Girl', in The Pump House Gang, *published in 1968.*

In San Francisco, Broadway is `the strip,' a combination of Macdougal Street in Greenwich Village and strip row on `East Bal'more' in Baltimore. It is about four blocks long, an agreeably goofy row of skin-show nightclubs, boho caves, saturated in black paint, with names like `Mother's', featuring light-projection shows, monologuists, intime jazz shows with brooding Negroes on the bass, and `colourful' bars with names like Burp Hollow. There is one tree on Broadway. It is about three inches in diameter, about 12 feet tall, and has 342 minute leaves on it and a tin anti-urine sleeve around the bottom.

A photograph of San Francisco taken in 1878 by English photographer Eadweard James Muybridge

The Sad Story of Jonestown

One of the weirdest stories associated with San Francisco is that of cult leader James Warren "Jim" Jones, who organized the mass-murder-suicide of over 900 people at Jonestown in Guyana in 1978. Jones was born in Indiana in 1931 and founded what was called the Peoples Temple. He was associated with both the Communist Party USA and the Methodist Church and in 1960, was appointed as head of the Indianapolis Human Rights Commission and worked to effect racial integration of businesses and hospitals in Indiana. In the meantime, he had married and adopted several children of non-Caucasian backgrounds, creating what he called a "Rainbow Family." Jones then moved to Brazil for several years before returning in 1963 when his People's Temple organization almost collapsed without his presence. He moved the Temple to California in the mid-1960s, and shifted the temple's headquarters to San Francisco in the early 1970s. In his speeches, he became increasingly clear that the message of the People's Temple was communism of a Soviet/North Korean/Maoist variety. "If you're born in capitalist America, racist America, fascist America, then you're born in sin," he said. "But if you're born in socialism, you're not born in sin." He began attacking Christianity and the Bible and declared that he was the reincarnation of Mahatma Gandhi, V.I. Lenin, Jesus and Buddha.

"What you need to believe in is what you can see," he was quoted as saying. "If you see me as your friend, I'll be your friend. As you see me as your father, I'll be your father, for those of you that don't have a father ... If you see me as your savior, I'll be your savior. If you see me as your God,

I'll be your God."

He lambasted Christianity, preaching: "There's only one hope of glory; that's within you! Nobody's gonna come out of the sky! There's no heaven up there! We'll have to make heaven down here!"

He became a political force in San Francisco, and helped George Moscone get elected as mayor in 1975. Moscone then appointed Jones as chairman of the San Francisco Housing Authority Commission. He met with vice presidential candidate Walter Mondale in 1976 and Mondale subsequently publicly praised the Temple. Rosalynn Carter, wife of President Jimmy Carter, also met with Jones on several occasions. At a huge dinner in Jones' honor in September 1977, California assemblyman Willie Brown gave a speech in which he praised Jones as "a combination of Martin King, Angela Davis, Albert Einstein... Chairman Mao."

But criticism of the Temple started to surface in the media and in mid-1977. Just before an expose article was to be published detailing abuses of members, Jones and several hundred Temple members moved to a Temple compound in Guyana in South America. Jones named the settlement "Jonestown." He had created it a few years earlier as an effort to create a "socialist paradise." "I believe we're the purest communists there are," he said.

He was still respected for his efforts at integration, and around two-thirds of Temple members were black. After the move to Jonestown, Jones increased his drug usage and started talking about how he and all his followers would die together and move to another planet and live happily ever after.

In November 1978, congressman Leo Ryan traveled with a team to Jonestown to investigate allegations of human rights abuses. His delegation included relatives of Temple members, an NBC camera crew and other media representatives. The visited Jonestown where Ryan was attacked by temple member with a knife. They left and went back to the airport, but were followed by members of Jones "Red Brigade" who opened fire on the delegation, killing Congressman Ryan and four others. Later that day, 909 inhabitants of Jonestown, 304 of them children, died of cyanide poisoning, mostly in and around the settlement's main pavilion. In a tape found after the deaths, Jones is heard telling Temple members that the Soviet Union had decided not to give the Temple members asylum, and he argued that everyone should commit suicide rather than allow themselves to be taken back to the US and converted into fascist dummies.

"We didn't commit suicide; we committed an act of revolutionary suicide protesting the conditions of an inhumane world," he added.

Jones died from a gunshot wound to the head. It is believed to have been self-inflicted.

Patty And The SLA

One of the weirdest stories of the 20th or any other century was that of Patty Hearst, the grand-daughter of the American publishing baron Randolph Hearst who was a student at University of California Berkeley in 1974. At the age of 19, she was kidnapped by a left-wing terrorist group called the Symbiomese Liberation Army. It was the age when Liberation Armies were active in San Francisco. She was placed in isolation where the group threatened to kill her and raped her several times. The SLA demanded a poverty and hunger relief program be created as a condition of her relief, and Patty's grand-father funded one.

Patty then shockingly declared that she had joined the SLA. In a tape released 59 days after her kidnapping, she declared: "I have been given the choice of being released...or joining the forces of the Symbionese Liberation Army and fighting for my freedom and the freedom of all oppressed people. I have chosen to stay and fight."

She further declared that she had taken the name "Tania," after a "comrade who fought alongside Che in Bolivia."

According to Hearst's later testimony, she spent a week blindfolded in a closet with her hands tied, during which time SLA leader DeFreeze repeatedly threatened

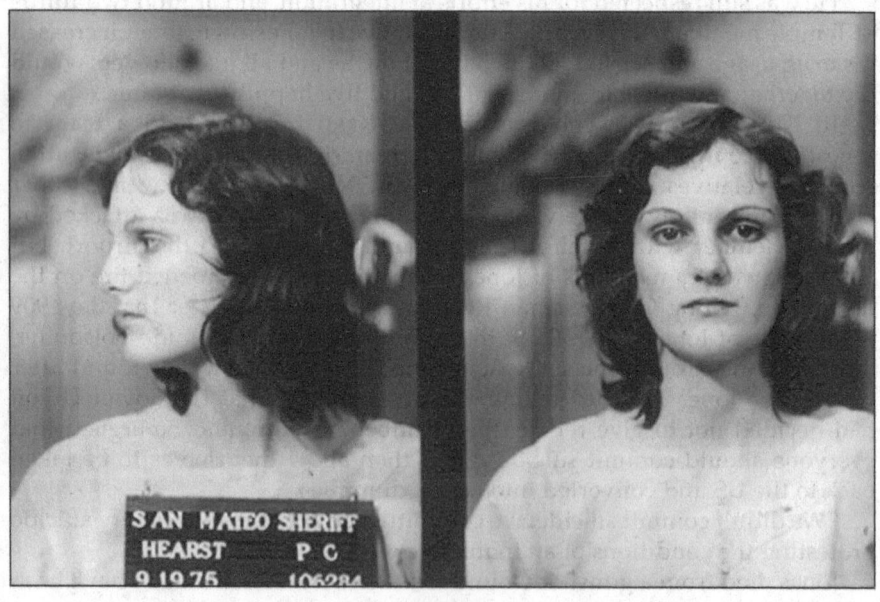

Patty Hearst

to kill her. But she gradually began to join in the group's political discussions, then was given a flashlight so she could read SLA political tracts in her closet. After several weeks, "DeFreeze told me that the war council had decided or was thinking about killing me or me staying with them, and that I better start thinking about that as a possibility. I accommodated my thoughts to coincide with theirs."

She participated in several crimes, including a bank robbery in which a woman was killed. Then 19 months after being kidnapped, she was found, or caught, or rescued, depending upon your point of view. She was tried and convicted of bank robbery, and sentenced to seven years in jail, but the sentence was commuted by President Jimmy Carter. She was pardoned by President Bill Clinton.

She later married one of the policemen responsible for guarding her, had two children and became an East Coast socialite.

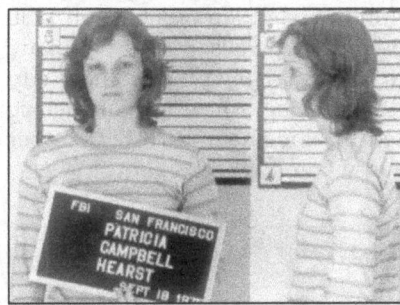

But oh, San Francisco! It is and has everything. You wouldn't think that such a place as San Francisco could exist. The wonderful sunlight there, the hills, the great bridges, the Pacific at your shoes. Beautiful Chinatown. Every race in the world. The sardine fleets sailing out. The little cable-cars whizzing down The City hills.The lobsters, clams, crabs. Oh, Cat, what food for you. And all the people are open and friendly.

Dylan Thomas, Welsh poet

The Castro

This is an area of San Francisco in Eureka Valley that gets its name from Castro Street, and the Castro Theatre, opened in 1922 with a Spanish baroque facade. The street and theatre are named after Jose Castro who tried hard and unsuccessfully to maintain Mexican control of California in the 1830s and 1840s. In the 1970s, the Castro became one of the world's largest and most prominent communities of gays and lesbians, bisexuals and transgenderites, and successfully led the way in terms of homosexuals "coming out," admitting their sexual orientation publicly, then facing the AIDS crisis that ravaged the gay community in the 1970s and 1980s.

The patron saint of the Castro is Harvey Milk, the first openly gay person ever to be elected to public office in the United States. He was born in 1930 and moved from New York to San Francisco in the 1960s, one of the many people looking for a new life in the city in that era. He won a seat as a city supervisor in 1977 and was instrumental in passing a new city ordinance protecting gay rights. He was assassinated in November 1978 by another city supervisor who had just lost his job and wanted it back again.

Boffo

Douglas Adams was an English novelest who created a wonderfully whacky series of books starting with the The Hitchhiker's Guide to the Galaxy. The Guide contained all sorts of strange information and tips, including an entry on San Francisco. Adams died at the age of 51 while working out in a gym in Santa Barbara, just south of San Francisco. This excerpt is from the last book in the series, So Long, *and* Thanks For All The Fish.

San Francisco, which the Guide describes as a "good place to go. It's very easy to believe that everyone you meet there is also a space traveller. Starting a new religion for you is just their way of saying `hi'. Until you've settled in and got the hang of the place it is best to say `no' to three questions out of any given four that anyone may ask you, because there are some very strange things going on there, some of which an unsuspecting alien could die of." The hundreds of curling miles of cliffs and sand, palm trees, breakers and sunsets are described in the Guide as "Boffo. A good one."

> The first thing that strikes the stranger in San Francisco is that it is built not upon fourteen hills but upon about ten thousand ladders.
> *A.G. Macdonell,* A Visit to America, *1935.*

An aerial photo of Alcatraz island in San Francisco, 1935

Read All About It!

San Francisco has been served by many newspapers over its history. Here are images of some of them.

San Francisco Chronicle

NORTHERN CALIFORNIA'S LARGEST NEWSPAPER

People

San Francisco has been the birthplace or home for far more than its fair share of prominent individuals. Here are some of them.

- Mel Blanc (1908–1989) - the voice of Bugs Bunny and more
- Jerry Brown (born 1938) - current and former Governor of California
- Pat Brown (1905–1996) - former Governor of California
- Willie Brown (born 1934) - Mayor of San Francisco, 1996–2004
- Herb Caen (1916-1997) - newspaper columnist
- Carol Channing (born 1921) - actress
- Francis Ford Coppola (born 1939) - film director, producer
- Isadora Duncan (1877–1927) - founder of Modern Dance
- Clint Eastwood (born 1930) - actor and film director
- Dianne Feinstein (born 1933) - San Francisco's first female mayor (1978–1988) and U.S. Senator since 1992
- Abigail Folger (1943–1969) - Folgers coffee heiress, murdered by Charles Manson's followers along with Sharon Tate and others
- Robert Frost (1874–1963) - poet
- Jerry Garcia (1942–1995) - guitarist, singer and Grateful Dead founder
- Gordon Getty (born 1934) - oil philanthropist and composer
- Danny Glover (born 1946) - actor
- Vince Guaraldi (1928–1976) - jazz pianist, writer of Peanuts theme
- Tom Hanks (born 1956) - actor
- William Randolph Hearst (1863–1951) - newspaper magnate
- Jim Jones (1931–1978) - cult leader, mass murderer
- Paul Kantner (born 1941) - co-founder of the band Jefferson Airplane
- Bruce Lee (1940–1973) - kung fu film star
- Jack London (1876–1916) - writer
- Courtney Love (born 1964) - Musician, actress and wife of Kurt Cobain
- George Lucas (born 1944) - film director and producer
- Armistead Maupin (born 1944) - writer, author of *Tales of the City* series of novels. Born in Washington D.C., but he deserves to be on this list
- Robert McNamara (1916–2009) - former Secretary of Defense
- Joe Montana (born 1956) - NFL quarterback for San Francisco 49ers
- Gordon Moore (born 1929) - co-founder of Intel Corporation and the author of Moore's law
- O. J. Simpson (born 1947) - NFL running back with San Francisco 49ers, actor and alleged murderer
- Natalie Wood (1938–1981) - actress

Tony Bennett, the singer most closely associated with San Francisco, was born in New York. Carlos Santana was born in Mexico, but his family moved to San Francisco when he was young, so he sort of counts. Joe diMaggio, the baseball player, was born in Martinez, but moved to San Francisco when he was just one year old. The rapper Tupac Shakur (1971-1996), was a resident of the Bay Area. Pop singer Johnny Mathis was born in Texas in 1935 but grew up in San Francisco.

A line of protestors picket outside of the St. Francis Hotel in San Francisco during the presidential campaign of Barry Goldwater. 1964

> You look back and see how hard you worked and how poor you were, and how desperately anxious you were to succeed, and all you can remember is how happy you were.
> *Jack London, novelist born in San Francisco*

Movies Set In San Francisco

The list of movies featuring the city is extremely long. Here selection.

- Barbary Coast
- Big Trouble in Little China
- Birdman of Alcatraz
- Born to Kill
- Bullitt
- Butterflies Are Free
- Chan Is Missing
- Charlie Chan at Treasure Island
- Chinatown at Midnight
- Chinatown Kid
- Chu Chu and the Philly Flash
- The Competition
- Confessions of an Opium Eater
- Dawn of the Planet of the Apes
- Days of Wine and Roses (film)
- Dim Sum: A Little Bit of Heart
- Dirty Harry
- Dr. Dolittle (film)
- Dragon Fight
- Dragon: The Bruce Lee Story
- The Enforcer
- Escape from Alcatraz
- The Falcon in San Francisco
- The Fatal Hour (1940 film)
- Flame of Barbary Coast
- Flower Drum Song (film)
- Fog Over Frisco
- Freebie and the Bean
- Frisco Jenny
- The Frisco Kid
- Godzilla
- Golden Gate (film)
- Golden Gate Girl
- The Graduate
- Guess Who's Coming to Dinner
- Harold and Maude
- The Heartbreak Kid (2007 film)
- Hello, Frisco, Hello
- The High and the Mighty (film)
- High Anxiety
- Homeward Bound II: Lost in San Francisco
- The House on Telegraph Hill
- Howl (film)
- The Woman on Pier 13
- Incident In San Francisco
- Innerspace
- Invasion of the Body Snatchers (1978 film)
- Final Days of Planet Earth
- The Jade Pussycat
- Jagged Edge (film)
- The Joy Luck Club (film)
- Kaleidoscope (1990 film)
- King of Alcatraz
- The Lady from Shanghai
- The Last Night of the Barbary Coast
- The Love Bug
- Magnum Force
- The Maltese Falcon (1941 film)
- Mega Shark Versus Giant Octopus
- Milk (film)
- La Mission (film)
- Mission: Impossible – Ghost Protocol
- Mr. Wong in Chinatown
- Mrs. Doubtfire
- No Escape (1953 film)
- Nob Hill (film)
- Northwest Hounded Police
- Old San Francisco
- Once a Thief (1965 film)
- The Organization (film)
- Out of the Past
- Outbreak (film)
- Play It Again, Sam (film)

- Playing Mona Lisa
- Point Blank (1967 film)
- Portrait in Black
- Possession (2009 film)
- The Presidio (film)
- Rise of the Planet of the Apes
- The Rock
- San Francisco (1936 film)
- The San Francisco Docks
- Shadows Over Chinatown
- Side Streets (1934)
- Star Trek
- The Strawberry Statement
- Street Fighter: The Legend of Chun-Li
- The Sweetest Thing
- Terminator Genisys
- Terminator Salvation
- They Call Me Mister Tibbs!
- The Three Stooges Go Around the World in a Daze
- The Towering Inferno
- Tweek City
- Vertigo (film)
- A View to a Kill
- What's Up, Doc?
- When a Man Loves a Woman (film)
- The Wild Parrots of Telegraph Hill
- The Woman in Red (1984 film)

Lunch at Johnny Kan's restaurant